Cambridge Elements ≡

Elements in the Global Middle Ages
edited by
Geraldine Heng
University of Texas at Austin
Susan J. Noakes
University of Minnesota–Twin Cities
Lynn Ramey
Vanderbilt University

"ETHIOPIA" AND THE WORLD, 330–1500 CE

Yonatan Binyam
Institute for Advanced Study

Verena Krebs
Ruhr-University Bochum

CAMBRIDGE
UNIVERSITY PRESS

Shaftesbury Road, Cambridge CB2 8EA, United Kingdom

One Liberty Plaza, 20th Floor, New York, NY 10006, USA

477 Williamstown Road, Port Melbourne, VIC 3207, Australia

314–321, 3rd Floor, Plot 3, Splendor Forum, Jasola District Centre, New Delhi – 110025, India

103 Penang Road, #05–06/07, Visioncrest Commercial, Singapore 238467

Cambridge University Press is part of Cambridge University Press & Assessment, a department of the University of Cambridge.

We share the University's mission to contribute to society through the pursuit of education, learning and research at the highest international levels of excellence.

www.cambridge.org
Information on this title: www.cambridge.org/9781009500982

DOI: 10.1017/9781009106115

© Yonatan Binyam and Verena Krebs 2024

This publication is in copyright. Subject to statutory exception and to the provisions of relevant collective licensing agreements, no reproduction of any part may take place without the written permission of Cambridge University Press & Assessment.

When citing this work, please include a reference to the DOI 10.1017/9781009106115

First published 2024

A catalogue record for this publication is available from the British Library.

ISBN 978-1-009-50098-2 Hardback
ISBN 978-1-009-10796-9 Paperback
ISSN 2632-3427 (online)
ISSN 2632-3419 (print)

Cambridge University Press & Assessment has no responsibility for the persistence or accuracy of URLs for external or third-party internet websites referred to in this publication and does not guarantee that any content on such websites is, or will remain, accurate or appropriate.

"Ethiopia" and the World, 330–1500 CE

Elements in the Global Middle Ages

DOI: 10.1017/9781009106115
First published online: May 2024

Yonatan Binyam
Institute for Advanced Study

Verena Krebs
Ruhr-University Bochum

Author for correspondence: Verena Krebs, verena.b.krebs@rub.de

Abstract: This Element offers an interdisciplinary introduction to the histories of the Ethiopian and Eritrean highlands from late antiquity to the late medieval period, updating traditional Western academic perspectives. Early scholarship, often by philologists and religious scholars, upheld "Ethiopia" as an isolated repository of ancient Jewish and Christian texts. This work reframes the region's history, highlighting the political, economic, and cultural interconnections of different kingdoms, polities, and peoples. Utilizing recent advancements in Ethiopian and Eritrean Studies as well as Medieval Studies, it reevaluates key instances of contact between "Ethiopia" and the world of Afro-Eurasia, situating the histories of the Christian, Muslim, and local-religious or "pagan" groups living in the Red Sea littoral and the Ethiopian-Eritrean highlands in the context of the Global Middle Ages.

Keywords: Ethiopia, Eritrea, global medieval history, Red Sea region, transcultural history

ISBNs: 9781009500982 (HB), 9781009107969 (PB), 9781009106115 (OC)
ISSNs: 2632-3427 (online), 2632-3419 (print)

Contents

Introduction

Although Ethiopian Studies within Western scholarship dates back to the middle of the seventeenth century, the field has long been dominated by philologists and scholars of religion. Their interest in premodern Ethiopian history stemmed largely from their perception of "Ethiopia" as a Christian nation and a reservoir of ancient Jewish and Christian works that had been lost to the West.

As a result, Western historiography traditionally emphasized the geographic and cultural isolation of Ethiopia, depicting it primarily as a Christian realm "cut off from medieval Europe by deserts, distance, and Islam" (Crawford 1958, 3). Recent scholarship has done much to correct such views. Textual, historical, archaeological, and encyclopedic projects have thoroughly revised long-held notions about the realms and peoples of the Ethiopian-Eritrean highland plateau and the Red Sea littoral. In the past decade, significant research conducted by teams from France, Germany, Italy, Ethiopia, and Eritrea has challenged and even overturned presumed scholarly "truths." This Element is an attempt to present an overview of this new state of scholarship on the various early realms once found in the territories of what are now the State of Eritrea and the Federal Democratic Republic of Ethiopia in the so-called medieval millennium, which we define as starting from the fourth century CE – the first appearance of Christianity in the region – to 1500 AD, roughly aligning with established Western academic concepts of late antiquity and the Middle Ages. We have consequently decided to put the "Ethiopia" in the title of this Element in quotation marks, first to acknowledge that much of the history covered therein takes place far beyond the borders of the modern nation-states (Ethiopia, Somaliland, Yemen, and Eritrea), and second because we hope that some of the (hi)stories presented in this Element will challenge commonly held notions on how "Ethiopia" has been understood and perceived in the field of Medieval Studies.

While we aim to offer a broad and introductory overview here, the brevity of this Element limits the topics we can cover. Historiography has long favored written sources over material culture, creating a bias toward well-documented Christian kingdoms at the expense of equally significant Muslim and local-religious or "pagan" realms. In fact, many of the people from "Ethiopia" that ventured forth into a wider world between 330 and 1500 CE – pilgrims, merchants, and especially the enslaved – have left us scarce records, making it challenging to reconstruct their histories or lived realities.

In keeping with some of the objectives of the Global Middle Ages Project, we still aim to inculcate "new habits of thinking" about Ethiopian history (Heng 2021, 6). The Element intentionally takes an interdisciplinary approach that strives to equally privilege written, archaeological, visual, and material culture sources to analyze political, economic, social, religious, and artistic issues as part of one mosaic. We also seek to problematize earlier models of periodization by highlighting how actors in various moments of Ethiopian-Eritrean history conceptualized their place in the world differently (Symes 2011, 716). Extending the Global Middle Ages paradigm, we show the occurrence of multiple premodernities in the history of this region, demonstrating the impossibility of accounting for a single and stable historical referent that can answer to the name "Ethiopia."

We have divided the Element into six sections. The first three sections, written by Yonatan Binyam, broadly cover the history of the ancient Aksumite kingdom. Section 1 presents an overview of Aksum's relations with its African, South Arabian, and Greco-Roman neighbors as it rose to be a major economic and political force in the ancient world. Section 2 surveys the Christianization of the Aksumite Empire in the fourth century, which further cemented the relations between Aksum and the Roman Empire. Section 3 relates the sixth-century expansions of Aksumite rule into South Arabia.

The subsequent sections, written by Verena Krebs, trace the histories of Christian, Muslim, and local-religious or "pagan" groups inhabiting the area extending from the Red Sea coast to the Ethiopian-Eritrean highland interior between the seventh and the fifteenth centuries. Section 4 surveys the fragmentary history of the post-Aksumite highlands and their connections to the Mediterranean and Red Sea regions. Section 5 traces the emergence of cosmopolitan Muslim and Christian polities tied into Fatimid trade networks stretching from the Maghreb to the Indian Ocean in the eleventh and twelfth centuries. Section 6 discusses the interplay of state formation, conquest, and trade in shaping the region's religious and political landscape until the arrival of the Ottomans and the Portuguese in the Horn of Africa in the sixteenth century.

1 The Emergence of the Aksumite Empire in Global Antiquity, Second–Fourth Centuries

As early as the fourth century, the term *Aethiopia* appears as a self-designating ethnonym in the ancient East African kingdom of Aksum, to which medieval and modern states identifying themselves as Ethiopia often trace their ancestry. Victory inscriptions dating to this century display the name of an Aksumite king and list the people groups under his control in two languages (Greek and Gǝʿǝz) and three scripts, with Gǝʿǝz written in both the Classical Ethiopic and the Pseudo-Sabaic scripts.[1] Here are the text and transliterations of three such inscriptions, together with a hybrid translation:[2]

> *ʾzn / ngś / ʾksm / [w]hmyr / wks / wsbʾ / whbśt / wrydn / wslh / wsym / wbg . . .* (Gǝʿǝz – *RIE* 185; *DAE* 7)

> *ʾzn / mlk / ʾksmm / wdhmrm / wrydnm / whbštm / wsbʾm / wslhm / wsymm / wksm / wbgm . . .* (Pseudo-Sabaic – *RIE* 185; *DAE* 6)

> Ἀζανᾶς Βασιλεὺς Ἀξωμιτῶν κα[ὶ] Ὁμηριτῶν καὶ τοῦ Ῥαειδᾶν καὶ Αἰθιόπων καὶ Σαβαειτῶν καὶ τοῦ Σιλεῆ καὶ τοῦ Τιαμῶ καὶ Βουγαειτῶν κ[αὶ] τοῦ Κάσου . . . (Greek – *RIE* 270; *DAE* 4)

> ʿEzana, king of the Aksumites, the Himyarites, the Raeidan, the Habashat/ Ethiopians, the Sabaeans, Silei (Salhen), Tiyamo, the Beja and the Kasu . . .

The Greek term *Aethiopia* here translates the term *hbśt* (or *hbšt* in the Pseudo-Sabaic script), the Semitic ethnonym variously used to refer to the people of Aksum, a larger group to which the Aksumites belonged, or subjects of Aksum residing in the Ethiopian-Eritrean highlands (Munro-Hay 1991, 15–16). Confusingly, the label *Aethiopia* is not applied consistently in the source materials dating from the ancient and late antique periods. For example, although the term is given as the equivalent of *hbśt* in the ʿEzana inscription cited just now, thus ostensibly referring to the Aksumites themselves or kindred groups, other Aksumite inscriptions from that time utilize *Aethiopia* to refer to the Nubian kingdoms located to the northwest of them (e.g. *RIE* 186).

Contemporaneous Greek and Roman texts mirror this ambivalence in the use of the term. On the one hand, *Aethiopia* frequently refers to Nubia in ancient Greek sources, including those dating to the Hellenistic and Roman periods. On the other hand, Greek authors come to adopt the self-designation of the Aksumites, and they too begin to refer to them as Ethiopians perhaps as early

---

[1] The use of two different scripts of Gǝʿǝz (Classical Ethiopic and Pseudo-Sabaic) was a common feature of fourth-century Aksumite inscriptions. In such cases, the same text would appear in Greek, an unvocalized Gǝʿǝz version utilizing the more cursive *fidäl* script of Classical Ethiopic (written from left to right), as well as a version in the unvocalized *musnad* script of epigraphic South Arabian, this last often also featuring Pseudo-Sabaic elements such as mimation and the use of north-Semitic cognates for Gǝʿǝz terms (e.g. *mlk* as opposed to *ngs* for "king"). For more, see Hatke 2013, 69; Phillipson 2014, 58.

[2] References to Aksumite inscriptions are here given by their designations according to the two standard catalogues, the *Deutsche Aksum-Expedition* (or *DAE*) and the *Recueil des inscriptions de l'Ethiopie des périodes axoumite et pré-axoumite* (or *RIE*). Unless otherwise indicated, numbers listed after *DAE* and *RIE* refer to an inscription and not a page number.

as the fifth century, as indicated in the epitome of Philostorgius's *Ecclesiastical History* (*Phil.* 3.6).[3] To complicate the matter further, in subsequent centuries, interpreters in the Ethiopic literary tradition begin to connect their country with references to Kush in the Hebrew Bible, a term translated as *Aethiopia* in Greek translations of biblical Hebrew texts. Later usages of "Ethiopia" thus flatten the complex topography of the term's usages in earlier periods.[4]

In view of this background, the Aksumite appropriation of the Greek *Aethiopia* in the fourth century appears to have been a politically strategic move (Hatke 2013, 52–53). By identifying themselves as rulers of Ethiopia, the Aksumite kings were utilizing a readily fungible topo/ethnonym within the Greek lingua franca of the day. Through their inscriptions, they styled themselves as ushering in a new "modernity," in the sense of the term proposed by Carol Symes, not as a designation for a certain historical period, but rather as the propogandist declaration of the dawning of a new, more sophisticated age (Symes 2011, 719). Understood in this sense, Aksumite rulers broadcast their reigns as ushering in an unprecedented epoch marked by the unification of vast territories in the Horn of Africa and South Arabia, the maintenance of peace, the building or improving of infrastructures, the regulation of trade networks, and the flow of cultural exchange.

Today, Aksum is a city located in central Tigray, the northernmost region in the modern nation-state of Ethiopia, a region that also demarcates the southwestern border of Eritrea. Archaeological data shows that human settlements around this area go back as far as the Late Stone Age, c. 10,000 BCE (Phillipson 2003, 4). Several sites also indicate that settlements bearing striking resemblance to South Arabian cultures are established in areas near Aksum by around 800–700 BCE (Phillipson 2014, 22–40). These settlements are characterized by architecture similar to that found in South Arabia, inscriptions in Gəʿəz utilizing modified forms of Sabaean script, and religious symbols bearing close affinities to South Arabian religions (Munro-Hay 1991, 106–202).

Aksum's advantageous location in close proximity to the Nile Valley, the Red Sea, and the Arabian Peninsula contributed to its growth into one of the most influential regional powerhouses in the ancient world. Over the course of centuries after the turn of the first millennium, it gradually emerged as a major political and commercial state, controlling large regions across the Horn of Africa and at times even straddling both sides of the Red Sea. Although it is difficult to pin down with precision exactly when and under what circumstances the rulers of Aksum began to expand the territories under their control,

---

[3] See Philostorgius 2007, 43.
[4] For an excellent discussion of the gradual association of the name *Aethiopia* with the Ethiopian-Eritrean highlands over the course of centuries, see Simmons 2022, 14–34.

a range of historical artifacts from written accounts to archaeological remains to epigraphic and numismatic evidence allows for the reconstruction of parts of the historical picture.

Aksum and International Trade in Antiquity

The earliest documentary witness to Aksum survives in the *Periplus of the Erythrean Sea* (or "The Circumnavigation of the Erythrean Sea"), the composition of which can confidently be dated to the middle of the first century (Bowersock 1971, 223). The title of the text is somewhat misleading, since, unlike earlier *periploi* that serve primarily as guides for sailors, the *Periplus of the Erythrean Sea* (hereafter *PES*) is a guide specifically for merchants, providing a description of the various commercial goods bought and sold in the major port cities and emporia along the Erythraean Sea.[5]

Furthermore, since the ancient designation literally means "Red Sea," the text is sometimes mistakenly viewed as a guide for trade on the Red Sea alone. However, at the time of the text's composition, "Erythraean Sea" referred not only to the Red Sea (which the text calls the Arabian Gulf [ὁ Ἀραβικὸς κόλπος]) but also to the Gulf of Aden and the western Indian Ocean (Casson 1989, 94). The international scope of the text's purview, therefore, extends beyond the Red Sea region and provides an invaluable glimpse into the major trading centers active in the first century CE from India to the Mediterranean.

The *PES* mentions Aksum in the context of discussing its major port city, Adulis, which lies a short distance inland from the Gulf of Zula on the East African coast of the Red Sea. The text indicates the significance of a given port in a number of different ways: one, by the number of times the port is mentioned; two, by noting the best seasons of the year to travel to said port; and three, by indicating the regulatory protocols governing trade at that location. In the first case, the *PES* mentions Adulis only a handful of times, in comparison to Barygaza of India, for example, which receives the most mentions at twenty-eight (Casson 1989, 277).

But the *PES* establishes the significance of Adulis as one of the most important centers of trade in the Indian Ocean market, initially by giving instructions about the best times of year to travel there. Out of a total of thirty-seven port cities, Adulis is one of only six cities (including Barygaza) for which

---

[5] For the standard text and translation of the *Periplus*, see Casson 1989. The text is preserved in a single manuscript dating to the tenth century: Codex Palatinus Graecus 398, fols. 40V–54V, in the Universitats Bibliothek, Heidelberg. Another manuscript dating to the fourteenth or fifteenth century and currently in the British Museum (B.M. Add. 19391, fols. 9r–i2r) is a direct copy of the Palatine manuscript, "errors and all" (Casson 1989, 5). Casson based his translation and commentary on the critical edition of the text compiled by Hjalmar Frisk in 1927.

the text provides seasonal travel guides, which would have been useful for merchants planning roundtrip voyages (6:3.4–7).[6] More distinguishing still is the description of Adulis as an *emporium nominom* (or "legal emporium"), one of only three port cities that the *PES* designates as such. The text then describes the connection between Adulis and Aksum as follows:

> On this part of the coast, opposite Oreine, twenty stades in from the sea is *Adulis* (ἡ Ἄδουλι), *a fair-sized village* (κώμη σύμμετρος). From Adulis it is a journey of three days to Koloe, an inland city that is the first trading post for ivory, and from there another five days *to the metropolis itself, which is called Axomites* (εἰς αὐτὴν τὴν μητρόπολιν τὸν Ἀξωμίτην λεγόμενον); into it is brought all the ivory from beyond the Nile through what is called Kyeneion, and from there down to Adulis (4:2.4–10).

The (albeit misspelled) reference to Aksum as the metropolis of Adulis indicates that the latter served as the major port for the former, similar to the relations linking Ostia to Rome (Bowersock 2013, 11). The *PES* paints a picture of Adulis as a vibrant trading center giving Aksumites an outlet to sell their goods (especially ivory and obsidian) and to purchase foreign goods of all kinds (e.g. articles of clothing, linens, drinking vessels, glass stones, brass, iron, copper, axes, knives, Roman money for resident foreigners, wine from Laodicea and Italy, olive oil, silverware, and goldware, to name but a few) (6:2.23–35).

The anonymous author describes some of the products (e.g. wine, olive oil) as "limited in quantity," other products (e.g. silverware and goldware) as goods purchased by the wealthy, and still others (e.g. unadorned clothing) as modest in price. In sum, the emporium available to the Aksumites is portrayed as a market for both the rich and those with modest means, who through Adulis had access to commodities from Italy, Greece, Egypt, Arabia, and India. In his *Natural History*, Pliny the Elder confirms this view of Adulis as a key emporium by describing it as "the biggest port . . . of the Ethiopians" (6.173).

As Lionel Casson has suggested, the designation of Adulis as an *emporium nominon* probably indicates that it was a "legally limited" port, meaning that all trade was regulated by the local governor or a trading office sanctioned by the ruler (Casson 1989, 276). The text also mentions a certain Zoskales, describing him as the king of the regions surrounding Adulis and "a fine person . . . well versed in reading and writing Greek" (5:2.19–21). Since Aksum is given as the metropolis of Adulis, numerous commentators have suggested that the Zoskales mentioned in the *PES* constitutes the first documented king of Aksum. By contrast, since the text

---

[6] Following Casson's method for numbering passages in the *PES*, references to the text here indicate the chapter followed by the page number(s), then line number(s) in Frisk's edition. Thus 6:3.4–7 = chapter 6, page 3, and lines 4–7.

explicitly refers to him as the king of Barbaria and not as king of Aksum, others have suggested that Zoskales was the ruler of a vast region in the Horn centered on Adulis but independent of (or perhaps even governing over) the city of Aksum (Casson 1989, 109–10). As a result of the ambiguities surrounding the connection between Zoskales and Aksum, it is not possible to reconstruct precisely the political extent of Aksumite rule in the Ethiopian-Eritrean highlands during the first century CE.

Aksumite Expansions in South Arabia

The earliest unambiguous reference to Aksumite expansions across the Horn of Africa and South Arabia appears in a now-lost victory inscription, which was once written on a commemorative throne but today survives only in the sixth-century *Topographica Christiana* of Cosmas Indicopleustes.[7] Cosmas is the medieval moniker given to an otherwise anonymous Nestorian Christian merchant who, in the sixth century, traveled to numerous places along the Red Sea, the Persian Gulf, and the Indian Ocean. He also visited Aksum around 518 CE (Hatke 2011, 79–80). He then wrote an annotated geography of the places he had visited some twenty-five years after his travels.

In his account, he relates that he came across a commemorative throne (*diphros* in Greek, as opposed to *thronos*), which had been enshrined "in Adulis ... the name of the city of the Ethiopians that ... serves as the port for the people of Aksum" (*Top. Chr.* 2.54). Cosmas's description of the votive throne is commonly referred to in the literature today as *Monumentum Adulitanum II*, together with *Monumentum Adulitanum I*, the designation for his description of a nearby stele that had been carved from a black rock (most likely basalt). While the marble throne had been erected in front of the basalt stele at the same location in Adulis, and both bore victory inscriptions written in Greek, they were not erected by the same ruler as Cosmas had thought (*Top. Chr.* 2.54.6–18). Instead, they enshrined the accomplishments of two rulers who lived centuries apart.

Cosmas's surviving transcription of these victory inscriptions demonstrates that the black stele, or *Monumentum Adulitanum I*, was much older and recounted the accomplishments of the Hellenistic ruler Ptolemy III, who reigned in Egypt between 246 and 222 BCE. By contrast, the inscription on the marble throne, or *Monumentum Adulitanum II*, related the victories of an Aksumite king whose reign most likely dates to the late second or early third century CE (Bowersock 2013, 56–57). The name of this Aksumite ruler has been lost, but, based on the territories he claims to have brought under his control, it is clear that he was not the same figure mentioned as Zoskales in the *PES*.

---

[7] For the text, see Wolska-Conus 1962.

In the inscription, the king boasts that he conquered numerous people groups who lived not only in the Horn region but as far north as the frontiers of Egypt and as far east as South Arabia across the Red Sea. The list of his military accomplishments concludes with the following words:

> I was the first and only king of any down to my time to subjugate all these peoples. That is why I express my gratitude to my greatest god, Ares, who also begat me, through whom I brought under my sway all the peoples who are adjacent to my land ... Having imposed peace on the entire world under me, I went down to Adulis to sacrifice to Zeus, to Ares, and to Poseidon on behalf of those who go under sail. Once I had brought together my forces and united them, I encamped in this place and made this throne as a dedication to Ares in the twenty-seventh year of my reign (*Top. Chr.* 2.63.8–12).

This inscription reveals several important points about the earliest period of Aksumite imperial expansion, as well as Aksum's relations with the other major powers of the ancient Mediterranean world. First, that the inscription was written in Greek indicates the Hellenization of Aksumite culture (at least across the more powerful levels of society), a process that may have begun as early as the third century BCE and definitely continued through to the Roman period, given the dating of the stele to the Ptolemaic period and the Aksumite throne to the second or third century CE. The unknown Aksumite king behind the Adulis throne here signals his command of Greek customs not only by mimicking the language of Ptolemy III as inscribed on the basalt stele but also by invoking Greek gods and describing himself as a son of Ares in terms that would have been widely intelligible to travelers acquainted with Greco-Roman religions and customs.

Second, *Monumentum Adulitanum II* represents the earliest surviving evidence for Aksumite conquests in South Arabia, as presented in the following claims of the unknown Aksumite king: "I sent both a fleet and an army of infantry against the Arabitai and the Kinaidocolpitai who dwell across the Red Sea, and I brought their kings under my rule ... I made war from Leukê Kômê to the lands of the Sabaeans" (*Top. Chr.* 2.62.4–9). The list of people and place names here indicates that the Aksumites took control of parts of the Arabian Peninsula from the port of Leukê Kômê in the north to the territories of the Sabaeans in the south, or, in modern terms, from the Gulf of ʿAqaba to the northern border of Yemen (Hatke 2013, 41). This account of the Aksumite takeover in South Arabia is corroborated by a fragmentary Greek inscription found at Aksum (i.e. *RIE* 269), which preserves the phrase "and the region across the sea" (καὶ τὸ πέρα τῆς θαλάσ[σης]), similar to the description in *Monumentum Adulitanum II* of the people living "across the Red Sea" (πέραν δὲ τῆς Ἐρυθρας θαλάσσης).

Arguably of more significance are parallel attestations of Aksumite rule that have been discovered among the surviving epigraphic evidence in South Arabia itself. A number of inscriptions indicate that Aksumites alternately invaded or made alliances with key South Arabian kingdoms like Saba' and Himyar during the first three quarters of the third century (Robin 1989). Several South Arabian inscriptions dating to this time period even provide the name of one Aksumite king, Gadara, leading some scholars to identify him as the ruler behind the throne inscription preserved in *Monumentum Adulitanum II* (Cuvigny and Robin 1996, 710–11).

In addition, the epigraphic evidence demonstrates that the Himyarites regain control of South Arabia beginning in the final quarter of the third century. The Aksumites appear to have been completely driven out from the Arabian Peninsula at this point, and no evidence of their presence is attested again in South Arabia until the first half of the sixth century (Hatke 2011, 119–76). The first wave of Aksumite rule in South Arabia can thus be more narrowly dated to c. 200–270 with relative confidence (Hatke 2013, 44). Despite their expulsion from the Arabian Peninsula by the close of the third century, Aksumite rulers continued to make irredentist claims to the other side of the Red Sea all the way through to the sixth century, as will be discussed in more detail in Sections 2 and 3.

Aksumite Expansions in Nubia

Third, *Monumentum Adulitanum II* also recounts Aksumite imperialist expansions northward from Aksum, from territories in the Ethiopian-Eritrean highlands surrounding the city to "as far as the frontiers of Egypt" (μέχρι τῶν Αἰγύπτου ὁρίων) (*Top. Chr.* 2.6). In his victory inscription, the unknown king further claims to have built "the road from the places of my kingdom all the way to Egypt" (τὴν ὁδὸν ἀπὸ τῶν τῆς ἐμῆς βασιλείας τόπων μέχρι Αἰγύπτου) (*Top. Chr.* 2.6). These claims seem to suggest that by extending Aksum's northern borders to Egypt, the Aksumite ruler had successfully invaded Nubia, which was located between his kingdom and Egypt. However, such a view is contradicted by the absence of any Nubian nations from the list of peoples he subjugated. Additionally, a number of Kushite inscriptions from around the middle of the third century suggest continued Nubian independence during this period (Hatke 2013, 48–59).

What the *Monumentum Adulitanum II* does indicate is the expansion of the kingdom's northern borders to encompass the Eastern Desert between the Nile and the Red Sea. This vast territory was inhabited by small tribes such as the Beja people, who appear in both Greco-Roman and Kushite sources, and are also listed in *Monumentum Adulitanum II* as one of the vassals of the Aksumite state (*Top. Chr.* 2.6). The non-Aksumite sources describe the Beja tribes as causing problems on Rome's southern and Nubia's eastern borders. It appears likely then that the Aksumite king sent his armies north to pacify his northern borders from the incursions of such tribes. By contrast, there is no evidence of a military struggle between the Nubian and Aksumite states during the third century.

Furthermore, the brief reference to a road between the Aksumite king's territories and Egypt indicates that part of his motivation was to facilitate trade and tribute collections via a land route. Nevertheless, commercial centers along the Nile Valley and the Red Sea would have continued to be the primary venues of Aksumite trade. Nubian kingdoms would no doubt have participated in this trade network, especially in the trade of iron and salt, for which there is some surviving archaeological evidence (Hatke 2013, 111). The absence of more evidence for trade between Nubia and Aksum most likely indicates that trade between the two kingdoms in this period primarily consisted in perishable goods (such as incenses, livestock, etc.), which do not survive in the archaeological record.

It is not until the first half of the fourth century that Aksum further extends its northern expansion by invading Nubia itself in two separate campaigns. Once again, the paucity of the surviving historical record severely limits the conclusions that can be drawn about the circumstances surrounding the outbreak of military conflict between Aksum and the kingdom on its northern border. However, a couple of victory inscriptions, the first on a monument erected at Aksum and the second in a fragmentary Greek text found at Meroe, together provide a low-resolution picture of the first Aksumite campaign against Nubia.

The two inscriptions evince that a certain Aksumite king invaded the Kushite capital of Meroe sometime in the first quarter of the fourth century. The inscription located in Aksum, referred to as *RIE* 186, features Kush (*Aethiopia* in Greek) in the list of vassals under Aksumite control. In contrast to *Monumentum Adulitanum II* where Aksumite sovereignty extends only up to the borders of Nubia/Ethiopia, in *RIE* 186 Kush/Ethiopia is depicted as a part of the Aksumite state. Additionally, the fragmentary inscription found in Meroe, catalogued as *RIE* 286, makes mention of an invasion by an Aksumite king who boasts of the patronage of the god Ares and appears to have imposed tribute on the conquered Nubians (Burstein 1981, 49).

Although the name of the king does not survive in either *RIE* 186 or the exceedingly lacunose *RIE* 286 fragment, several factors suggest that Ousanas (who ruled Aksum c. 310–330 CE) is most likely the ruler in question. Numismatic evidence dating to the 320s, featuring gold coins minted by

Ousanas, demonstrates that he ruled Aksum during the first quarter of the fourth century (Hahn 2000, 290; Munro-Hay 1991, 15). In several different victory inscriptions found at Aksum, furthermore, Ousanas is listed as the father of ʿEzana, who launches the second military campaign against Nubia. As will be discussed in Section 2, ʿEzana is the first Aksumite king to feature Christian symbols and language on his coins and victory inscriptions. The description of his campaign against Nubia, preserved in several inscriptions, reveals that he undertakes only one invasion of Nubia. Since the king who directs the first invasion associates himself with Ares, as evinced by *RIE* 286, it is most likely the case that his reign and invasion of Nubia precede those of ʿEzana.

In summary, the surviving record of written, epigraphic, and numismatic evidence suggests that Aksumite rulers began to expand the territories under their control as early as the late second or early third century. In addition to conquests over large swaths of the Ethiopian-Eritrean highlands and sur-rounding regions, the first stage of Aksumite expansions saw the short-lived annexation of South Arabia into the East African kingdom in the third century. This was followed in the fourth century by Aksumite invasions of Nubian kingdoms to the north of Aksum. The primary impetus for these campaigns was economic: in addition to extracting tributes from their subjects, Aksumite rulers sought to control key trade routes proximate to their capital city that flowed along the Nile Valley and through the crucial nexus between Africa and Asia along the Red Sea.

To this end, they positioned themselves as major players in the Greco-Roman *oikumene* by adopting the Greek language and depicting themselves on their coins and inscriptions in the widely recognizable style of Roman emperors. They also adopted Greco-Roman customs in order to more effectively substan-tiate their alliance with Rome. They did this most conspicuously by inserting themselves and their country, renamed to be familiar to Greek speakers, into the religious narratives of the Greco-Roman world. This Aksumite practice of mirroring Rome's religions and customs continued in the fourth century and beyond after the conversion of Roman emperors to the Christian religion.

2 Aksum in the World of Roman Late Antiquity, Fourth Century

The early adoption of Christianity in late antique East Africa is perhaps more renowned than any other feature of ancient Ethiopian history. Debates continue over the question of whether or not Ethiopia should be considered the first Christian nation, with some arguing that it merits the title over Armenia (Portella and Woldegaber 2012). The traditional accounts of the Ethiopian-Eritrean Orthodox churches push the date of the Ethiopian adoption of Christianity even earlier to the first century, relying on the story of the conversion of the Ethiopian eunuch as related in the New Testament. However, evidence from Greek and Roman sources suggests that in the first century the term *Aethiopia* more often than not referred to the kingdom of Meroe, the female rulers of which were known by the title given in Acts 8.27, namely Kandake (Gaventa 1986, 103). Consequently, most scholars interpret the allusion to Ethiopia in the Book of Acts as a reference to a Nubian kingdom, prior to the Aksumite appropriation of the term *Aethiopia*.

In contrast to the lack of evidence for Aksumite Christianity in the first century, an unusually substantial number of written, epigraphic, and numismatic sources illustrate the increasingly widespread adoption of Christianity in the kingdom of Aksum beginning in the first half of the fourth century. The account of Christianity's arrival in Aksum that appears in the fifth-century Latin *Ecclesiastical History* of Rufinus (c. 345–410) has become arguably the most famous version of the story.[8]

In his report, Rufinus never specifically mentions Aksum, or even Ethiopia, instead referring to the region as India, a common synonym for *Aethiopia* in ancient Greek and Latin texts. His account allocates all the agency behind the Aksumite conversion to Christianity to Frumentius, a Syrian refugee who ostensibly ends up in Aksum after being captured from a merchant's ship. Rufinus claims that Frumentius "promoted the seed of Christianity in the country" by facilitating the construction of Christian conventicles throughout the kingdom (*Hist. Eccles.* 10.9–10). He further adds that after being designated the "bishop in India," Frumentius converted "a countless number of barbarians" there to Christianity by performing "apostolic miracles" (*Hist. Eccles.* 10.9–10).

Despite the confessional nature of his report, scholarship on the question of Aksum's adoption of Christianity has been hampered by an overreliance on Rufinus's account, as well as by a failure to incorporate the Aksumite turn to Christianity within a broader view of contemporaneous trends in the late antique world. The present section aims to provide a corrective to these shortcomings by centering more reliable sources and by framing the Aksumite adoption of Christianity within a discussion of the sociopolitical and economic developments stemming from this seismic cultural shift, thus contextualizing the emergence of Aksumite Christianity within a global stage. In particular, it spotlights the connections between Aksum's adoption of Christianity and similar episodes of state adoptions of monotheistic cults, in addition to demonstrating the links between religious propaganda, internal state politics, and international alliances.

---

[8] For the text, see J.-P. Migne, ed. Rufinus, *Historia Ecclesiastical* (Migne 1849, 478–80). See also the translation by Philip R. Amidon (Rufinus 1997, 18–23).

Recent works from a number of different disciplines are continuing to develop more dynamic models for articulating and conceptualizing the cultic forms and sociopolitical functions of religions in late antiquity. In part, these studies attempt to account for the dramatic explosion in the popularity of monotheistic religions, which culminated in the globalizations of Christianity and Islam (e.g. Stroumsa 2015). A close examination of the various events that play a role in the growth of monotheistic cults reveals a complex and interconnected web of numerous sociopolitical, cultural, and economic factors. In order to highlight the enormous complexity of these interrelated phenomena, scholars have proposed a number of fluid categories such as pagan monotheism, henotheism, and megatheism (Chaniotis 2010; Mitchell and van Nuffelen 2010).

Models like pagan monotheism, henotheism, and megatheism are intended to capture the fact that around the same time as Aksum's conversion to Christianity, various states were adopting and promoting monotheistic cults in places where polytheism was prevalent (Mitchell and van Nuffelen 2010, 16–33). These episodes reveal that as a local community or regional kingdom's foreign relations become more critical to sustaining its economy and material conditions, supreme deities that can transcend the parochialism of local cults become useful totems for forging political bonds. During these moments, the formation of sociopolitical alliances across regional and/or national boundaries can be facilitated or even amplified by the governing powers.

In such cases of religious statecraft, monotheistic (or megatheistic) cults played a dual role politically. First, in what may be termed *state monotheism*, they functioned to stabilize domestic politics by serving as propagandist tools that could legitimize claims to sovereignty made by victorious generals in order to unify disparate populations under one polity. Second, in what is discussed later as *diplomatic monotheism*, they functioned to facilitate international relations, by creating a shared religious grammar that could underwrite sociopolitical alliances between neighboring political entities.

Both types of strategic use of religion are demonstrated in Aksumite inscriptions and coins dating to the fourth century, and it is possible to examine the links between state and religion through an analysis of Aksum's first Christian king, ʿEzana. Fortunately for historians, a substantial amount of written, epigraphic, and numismatic evidence for the reign of ʿEzana has survived. In fact, no other figure in Aksumite history is attested more widely in the surviving record than the first ruler to adopt Christianity. Three of his victory inscriptions illustrate the significance of religious symbolism for Aksumite rulers who sought to legitimize their rules, unify the various tribes in their kingdoms, and consolidate their international alliances. A fruitful approach to analyzing the phenomenon of Aksumite religious statecraft is to compare it with parallel trends that took place around the same time in the Roman Empire, beginning with Constantine I (r. 312–337).

Military Cults in Aksumite Religious Statecraft

The first set of 'Ezana's inscriptions under consideration here survives in both Gə'əz and Greek and appears to have been inscribed prior to his adoption of monotheism and his conversion to Christianity. The opening words of these inscriptions reveal that, at the time of their composition, 'Ezana maintained the Aksumite custom of promoting a war god, who is enshrined in both Gə'əz and Greek theonyms as illustrated below:

> *'zn / ngś / 'ksm / [w]hmyr / wks / wsb' / whbśt / wrydn / wslh / wsym / wbg / ngś / ngśt / wld / mhrm / ytmw'* ... (Gə'əz – *RIE* 185; *DAE* 7)

> Ἀζανᾶς Βασιλεὺς Ἀξωμιτῶν κα[ὶ] Ὁμηριτῶν καὶ τοῦ Ῥαειδᾶν καὶ Αἰθιόπῶν καὶ Σαβαειτῶν καὶ τοῦ Σιλεῆ καὶ τοῦ Τιαμῶ καὶ Βουγαειτῶν κ[αὶ] τοῦ Κάσου βασιλεὺς βασιλέων υἱὸς θεοῦ ἀνικήτου Ἄρεως ... (Greek – *RIE* 270; *DAE* 4)

> 'Ezana, king of the Aksumites, the Himyarites, the Raeidan, the Habashat/ Ethiopians, the Sabaeans, Silei (Salhen), Tiyamo, the Beja and the Kasu, king of kings, son of the invincible god Mahrem/Ares ...

This bilingual inscription, as preserved in *RIE* 185 and 270, shares some remarkable similarities with the strategies of legitimation employed by Constantine I during his military campaigns of the second and third decades of the fourth century, during which he fought to overtake the empire as sole ruler. Prior to his own famous conversion to Christianity, Constantine celebrated his military victories by minting coins in honor of Sol Invictus, the Unconquered Sun. By the fourth century, the cult of Sol Invictus had gained a large following among Rome's armies, which had become much more powerful since they increasingly determined who would ascend to the throne during the so-called crisis of the third century. Constantine's veneration of Sol Invictus followed on the heels of earlier Roman generals, from Aurelian (r. 270–275) to his father Constantius I (r. 286–306), both of whom promoted the cult of Sol Invictus in order to secure the loyalties of Rome's legions (Stephenson 2009, 62–86).

The Roman example demonstrates that rulers whose sovereignty was critically tied to the support of their armies were heavily invested in elevating the cults widely understood to be associated with military victories. This is the strategy employed in 'Ezana's bilingual inscription just now, wherein he broadcasts himself as the son of the invincible god (*ytmw'* in Gə'əz and ἀνικήτου in Greek), whose name is given as Mahrem for the Gə'əz-speaking domestic audience, and as Ares for the Greek-speaking foreign audience. The parallel attributions of invincibility to Sol Invictus and Mahrem may further indicate the function of these two state cults as particularly sacred for the respective armies of Rome and Aksum. Thus, although the earlier monuments of ʿEzana and Constantine do not exhibit any explicitly monotheistic beliefs, they nevertheless demonstrate the significance of religious symbols for securing and maintaining state power by martial means.

Additionally, ʿEzana's association of his reign with the more widely recognizable god Mahrem may have allowed him to transcend localized tribal traditions among his soldiers. That his army was organized along distinct clan lines is demonstrated by internal evidence from another one of his inscriptions, namely *RIE* 189, which provides a list of the different divisions within his army (Hatke 2013, 114–15). Given that the Aksumite military force was made up of coalitions from different tribes with ostensibly different religious traditions, ʿEzana's veneration of a high god that could transcend local differences would have been quite useful as a strategy of religious statecraft. Although the evidence is much too sparse to allow reconstructing the Aksumite pantheon and cosmology, the surviving record suggests that high gods like Asthar and Mahrem appear to have been worshipped throughout the Horn region and in South Arabia by this time (Munro-Hay 1991, 196–98).

ʿEzana's Invasion of Nubia

In contrast to *RIE* 185, ʿEzana's two other victory inscriptions under consideration here, *RIE* 189 and *RIE* 271, both evince a radical shift in his strategies of religious statecraft. Internal evidence suggests that *RIE* 189 and 271 were produced around the same time, since they both memorialize the same event, namely ʿEzana's successful conquest of various tribes throughout the Nubian kingdom north of Aksum.[9] That the two inscriptions both attest to the same military expedition is demonstrated in part by the reason outlined in each as the *casus belli* that impelled the Aksumite king to launch a campaign against Nubia.

In both *RIE* 189 and 271, ʿEzana states that he went north with his armies in response to pleas for aid from various peoples, who were under attack by a tribe referred to as the Noba. Based on the appellation given to them in these inscriptions, the Noba appear to have been a group of Nubian-speaking tribes who had settled along the Nile in Upper Nubia and were viewed by the Aksumites as distinct from the Meroitic-speaking Kushites, whom they were attacking (Hatke 2013, 82). In *RIE* 189 we find not only the names of some of

---

[9] There is also a third inscription that relates the same campaign, *RIE* 190, written in unvocalized Gəʿəz script.

the Noba tribes that the Aksumite armies subdued but also indications of the geographical extent of ʿEzana's conquests; he claimed to have successfully marched as far as the confluence of the ʿAtbara and the main Nile, which lay almost 100 kilometers north of Meroe (Hatke 2013, 116).

The unusually well-preserved accounts of ʿEzana's conquests in Nubia are valuable for the details that they provide about the sociopolitical and economic conditions in the region at that time. In particular, *RIE* 189 lists livestock, grain, copper, cotton, and iron as some of the commodities that the Aksumites confiscated in the course of their invasion. The mention of iron in ʿEzana's inscriptions corroborates the archaeological evidence excavated in Kushite sites such as Meroe, Tabo, and Napata, which suggests the immense significance of iron mining and forging for the regional economy. By some estimates, the area may have seen an annual production of between 5 and 20 tons of iron objects over the course of 500 years (Haaland and Haaland 2007, 380–81).

Cotton had also become an important commodity during the Roman period, by which point Nubians were using it for the production of textiles (Chowdhury and Buth 1971; Wild et al. 2007). The capture of tens of thousands of sheep, oxen, and camels described in *RIE* 189 further attests to the centrality of livestock for the regional economy, which aligns with the fact that the rich soil adjacent to the Nile would have allowed for the grazing of large herds.

While they parallel one another in their descriptions of ʿEzana's military campaigns in Nubia, *RIE* 189 and *RIE* 271 propagandize the resulting victories in two starkly different religious grammars. The first, *RIE* 189, espouses a generic monotheism (or megatheism) directed internally to Aksum's non-Christian inhabitants. The second, *RIE* 271, promotes explicitly Christian beliefs aimed outwardly toward the newly Christian empire of the Romans. The contrasting religious grammars that characterize *RIE* 189 and *RIE* 271 indicate that ʿEzana sought to enshrine his military victories and declare his political ambitions in terms that would have simultaneously appealed to both a domestic and a foreign audience. Not incidentally, the first inscription is written in Gəʿəz, and the latter in Greek.

Empire Building and Monotheism in Aksumite Religious Statecraft

In the Gəʿəz inscription, ʿEzana attributes his successes to an unspecified deity referred to variously as "Lord of Heaven" (*'egziʾa samay*), "Lord of Earth" (*'egziʾa medr*), and "Lord of All" (*'egziʾa kwelu*), as partially illustrated in this quotation:

[ba]hayla / ʿegziʾa / samay / [zaba] / samay / wamedr / mawaʾi / lita / ʾana /
ʾe[za]na / walda / ʾele / ʾamida / beʾeseya / halen / negusa / ʾaksum / waza /
heme[r] / waza / raydan / waza / sabaʾ / waza / salhen / waza / seyamo / waza /

*bega / wa[za] / kasu / neguśa / nagaśt / walda / 'ele / 'amida / za'ayetmawā' /
lasar / [baha]yla / 'egzi'a / samāy / zawahabani / 'egzi'a / kwelu / zabot[u] /
a[man][ku / negu]ś / za'ayetmawā / lasar . . .* (Gə'əz – *RIE* 189; *DAE* 11)

> By the power of the Lord of Heaven who is in heaven and [on] earth, the
> Victorious, I 'Ezana son of Ǝllä 'Amida, the man of the Halen [Clan], King of
> Aksum, Himyar, Raiedan, Saba, Salhen, Seyamo, the Beja and Kush, king of
> kings, son of Ǝllä 'Amida, unconquered by the enemy. By the power of the
> Lord of Heaven who has given to me, the Lord of All in whom I believe, the
> king unconquered by the enemy . . .

The first of several striking features of this inscription is the absence of any
proper names of deities, which typically appear in Aksumite inscriptions
dating from earlier periods. In place of references to specific theonyms, *RIE*
189 alludes in places to a vague monotheism (or megatheism). Furthermore,
it contains no explicitly Christian language whatsoever, despite being produced around the same time as its Christian counterpart, *RIE* 271. The
absence of Christian expressions in an inscription that dates from the same
time period as Aksum's first Christian monument has led some scholars to
postulate an intermediary stage in 'Ezana's religious beliefs, in which he
ostensibly subscribed to a generic monotheism in the course of his multi-
stage conversion from polytheism to Christianity (e.g. Kaplan 1982).
Leaving aside the imagined religiosity of an individual ruler, it is possible
to interpret *RIE* 189 as political propaganda directed at a local non-Christian
population.

First, the inscription is written in Gə'əz, a language that would have been
legible only to local and regional inhabitants. Aksumite inscriptions antedating
those of 'Ezana are almost invariably characterized by their multilingualism,
demonstrating that they were intended to be read by both locals and foreigners.
By contrast, the monolingualism of *RIE* 189 suggests a more targeted audience,
one that would have been local or regional. This Gə'əz-speaking population
would not have subscribed to the foreign cults of the Romans, but would most
likely have been favorable toward the promotion of a supreme deity, such as the
one envisioned in *RIE* 189. In contrast to later readings of *RIE* 189 as a reference
to Christianity, it was most likely the case that 'Ezana's monotheistic inscription
would have been interpreted in pagan terms on the domestic front (Mekouria
1981, 405; Sergew Hable Selassie 1972, 105).

Second, 'Ezana's expansionist title for himself, *negusa negast* ("king of kings"),
demonstrates the continued Aksumite interest in establishing sociopolitical
cohesion throughout the kingdom, which arguably explains his promotion of
a monotheistic cult. As studies of the phenomenon of monotheism and its sociopolitical ramifications have suggested, the popularities of monotheistic cults often

correlate with the unification of disparate communities. Such moments of unification are sometimes the products of policies enacted by a state apparatus, and at other
times result from the sociocultural interconnections made possible by regional and
long-distance trade networks.

This phenomenon can be seen specifically in the African context, for
example, wherein local cults evince a growing emphasis on a high god in
correlation with the local community's increasing reliance on trade over subsistence farming (Horton 1971, 482). Even more specifically in the East African
context, there is evidence across the greater Horn region for the dual presence of
polytheistic cults with a monotheistic bent during the late antique period
(Levine 2000, 66). From this perspective, *RIE* 189 arguably evinces an example
of state monotheism, demonstrating 'Ezana's efforts to popularize
a monotheistic (or megathistic) cult with the goal of promoting unity throughout
the Horn region, while still allowing for local diversity.

Diplomacy and Christianity in Aksumite Religious Statecraft

'Ezana's state monotheism as reflected in the Gəʿəz *RIE* 189 contrasts sharply
with the diplomatic monotheism of the Greek *RIE* 271, which represents the
first Aksumite inscription to feature explicitly Christian language:

Ἐν τῇ πιστι τοῦ θ[εοῦ καὶ τ]ῇ δυνάμι τοῦ [πα]τρὸς καὶ υἱοῦ καὶ [ἀ]γί[ο]υ [π]
νεύματος, τ[ῷ] [σ]ώσαντι μοι τὸ βας[ίλ]ιον τῇ πίστι τοῦ υἱ[οῦ] αὐτοῦ Ἰησοῦ
χριστοῦ τῷ βοηθήσαντί μο[ι] τῷ καὶ πάντοταί μοι βοηθοῦντι ἐγὼ Ἀζανᾶς
βασιλεὺς Ἀξωμιτῶν καὶ Ὀμηρι[τῶν κ]αὶ τοῦ Ῥεειδᾶν καὶ Σαβαειτῶν καὶ τοῦ
Σ[ιλ]εῆλ καὶ τοῦ Χάσω καὶ Βουγαειτῶν [κ]αὶ τοῦ Τιαμῶ, Βισι Ἀλην, υἱὸς
τοῦ Ἑλλε-αμιδα, δοῦλος Χριστοῦ, εὐχαριστῶ Κυρίῳ τῷ [θεῷ] μου ... ὅτι ἐπ
[οί]ησεν ἐμοὶ ἠσχὺν καὶ δύναμιν καὶ ἐχαρίσ[α]τό μοι ὄ[ν]ομα μέγα διὰ τοῦ
υἱοῦ [α]ὐτοῦ εἰς ὃν ἐπ[ι]στευσα ... (*RIE* 271)

By faith in God and by the power of the Father and the Son and the Holy Spirit,
to him who has saved my kingdom through faith in his son Jesus Christ, to him
who helped me and who always helps me: I, 'Ezana, King of the Aksumites, the
Himyarites, the Raeidan, the Sabaeans, and of Salhen, Kush, the Beja, and of
the Seyamo, man of Halen, son of Ǝllä 'Amida, servant of Christ, thank the
Lord my God ... because he gave me strength and power and bestowed on me
a great name through his son in whom I have placed my faith ...

The diplomatic orientation of *RIE* 271 is in part demonstrated by the use of
Greek instead of Gəʿəz. The Greek text featured in the Aksumite inscriptions
antedating 'Ezana's typically translate what is written in Gəʿəz more or less
directly, with the important exception of renaming Aksumite gods using Greek
theonyms. By contrast, even though it is memorializing the same event as *RIE*
189, *RIE* 271 does not represent a translation of the former. Instead, it replaces

the vague monotheism of *RIE* 189 with explicitly Christian symbolism, indicating a deliberate re-presentation of 'Ezana's political accomplishments and goals in terms that would curry favor with Christian foreigners. Furthermore, 'Ezana probably had his foreign audience in mind when he chose to leave out the phrase *negusa negast* ("king of kings"), which appears in the Gə'əz *RIE* 189 but is curiously absent from the Greek *RIE* 271.

The epigraphic evidence for 'Ezana's adoption of Christianity is corroborated by the numismatic evidence. The surviving record of Aksumite coins indicates that the kingdom minted coins of various bases (e.g. gold, silver, copper) beginning in the late third century and continuing until the first half of the seventh century (Hahn 2016, 52). Similar to the political function of monumental inscriptions in the ancient world, coins were also valuable tools for the dissemination of royal propaganda, which once again was relayed through a religious vocabulary.

The earliest surviving coins demonstrate that Aksumite kings legitimized their reigns by casting their images on coins alongside symbols of the disc and the crescent. 'Ezana changes this practice in the early fourth century, after which point the cross comes to replace the disc and the crescent on Aksumite coins. In fact, since some of his Christian coins date from before the reform of the Roman currency by Constantine in 324 CE, 'Ezana may have been the first ruler anywhere in the world to imprint royal coins with the cross (Munro-Hay 1991, 190).

On the one hand, 'Ezana's promotion of Christianity constitutes a remarkable break from the customary formulas of Aksumite royal cults. On the other hand, however, it can be viewed as a continuation of the diplomatic strategy of aligning Aksumite religions with Greco-Roman ones. As already noted, several surviving inscriptions present the primary South Arabian gods worshipped in Aksum in both Semitic and Greek theonyms. For example, Astar the high god is rendered in Greek as Zeus, Mahrem as Ares, and Beher may have been associated with Poseidon (Munro-Hay 1991, 196–97). The tandem presentation of deities in Semitic and Greek theonyms would most likely have had the effect of strengthening diplomatic ties and fostering a level of cultural hybridity between Aksum itself and Rome's provinces.

One example that illustrates the sociopolitical ties forged by the Christianization of Aksum is a diplomatic letter sent to the Aksumite king from Constantius II, one of the sons of Constantine who ruled in Constantinople between 337 CE and 361 CE (Rukuni 2021). In his letter, Constantius voices his concerns over the "orthodoxy" of Aksumite Christianity and signals his desire to correct this problem by having the patriarch in Alexandria send a new bishop to Aksum (*Apologia* 31.13–17).[10]

---

[10] See the text edited by Jan M. Szymusiak (Athanasius 1987, 161).

Far from being an exclusively religious problem, the Arian controversy had become one of the most intractable political problems for Roman emperors of the fourth and fifth centuries. The letter of Constantius II suggests that Aksum not only was in regular contact with Alexandria and Constantinople but also was considered an important ally for the emperor to have on his side. Aksum's need to signal its doctrinal position during the nascent stages of Christian orthodoxy may have also been the reason behind the promotion of the Trinitarian formula of the Father, the Son, and the Holy Spirit in *RIE* 271.

In conclusion, a reading of Aksumite coinage and inscriptions dating to the fourth century reveals the dramatic changes in strategies of religious state-craft employed by the kingdom's first Christian king. 'Ezana found in Christianity a religious grammar with which he could address multiple political concerns at once, both within his kingdom and abroad. The inscrip-tions he left behind suggest that he was invested in retaining the loyalties of the armies under his command by promoting the cult of a war god, creating a cohesive society through the promotion of a monotheist (or megatheist) god, and signaling his diplomatic alliances by presenting his patron gods in both Ethiopic and Greek theonyms.

Christianity provided 'Ezana a way to accomplish all three political objectives through a unified religious system. It is probably no coincidence then that his adoption of Christianity in Aksum dates to the same time period as Constantine's adoption of Christianity in Rome, arguably making it another case of *imitatio imperii Romani*. Since the most powerful empire of 'Ezana's day had begun to promote the Christian cult, following Constantine's lead in declaring Christ his god would have substantiated Aksum's alliance with Rome. The monotheistic nature of Christianity also meant that, as the Romans adopted a new account of who they were as a people, the Aksumites could inscribe the narrative of their kingdom within that emerging ethnomyth in a much more homogeneous way than had previously been possible. Monotheism also rendered the royal or martial cult obsolete, since Christ came to replace Mahrem/Ares and Sol Invictus in Aksum and Rome, respectively, as the guarantor of military victories and the symbol of divine right to kingship.

'Ezana's interpolation of the myth of Ethiopia into the wider story of global Christianity would come to have significant consequences for the sociopoliti-cal destinies of the nation over the course of subsequent centuries. As Section 3 discusses, a number of conflicts that take place during the sixth century serve to deepen the political and diplomatic ties between the Romans and the Aksumites.

3 Aksum and South Arabia, Sixth Century

Similar to ʿEzana before him, the sixth-century Aksumite ruler Kaleb (or Ǝllä Aṣbəḥa) oversaw the expansion of Aksumite territories and strategically framed his military victories and political ambitions in religious language. While ʿEzana had expanded Aksum's borders to the north by invading Nubia, Kaleb stretched the boundaries of the kingdom to the east by invading South Arabia across the Red Sea. By the time the latter was able to reassert Aksumite control in South Arabia, a rival kingdom had emerged in Himyar as a regional power to contest the expansionist ambitions of Aksum. The sixth-century wars between Aksum and Himyar demonstrate how the Red Sea kingdoms were entangled with and critical to the geopolitical conflicts dominating the late antique world. They also illustrate how Aksumite rulers like Kaleb situated themselves within the geopolitics of the day by leveraging their Christianity and alliance with the Roman Empire. The world that Aksum helped shape in sixth-century Arabia further laid the groundwork for the emergence of the Islamic dynasties beginning in the seventh century.

As discussed in Section 1, the different tribes inhabiting South Arabia had first been made subjects of Aksum in the third century, before the Aksumites were expelled from the Peninsula sometime around 270 CE. The Aksumite retreat from South Arabia coincided with (and thus was most likely precipitated by) the consolidation of regional power by the emerging kingdom of Himyar. Around the turn of the fourth century, Himyar forged a unified kingdom out of what had previously been a collection of disparate tribes and kingdoms in South Arabia, including the kingdoms of Saba and Hadramawt (Grasso 2023, 71). The kings of Himyar began to broadcast their control of the region by advancing their royal titles through their monumental inscriptions, wherein they referred to their kingships over the Himyarites, the Raeidan, and the Sabaeans, in direct opposition to the same claims being made by Aksumite kings like ʿEzana across the Red Sea.

Furthermore, in line with broader trends that saw the strategic politicizing of monotheism across numerous parts of the late antique world like Aksum and Rome, monotheistic cults began to emerge in South Arabia as well during the fourth and fifth centuries. A century or so after the Himyarites first consolidated power in the region, their inscriptions began to propagate monotheistic beliefs rooted in Judaism, in a contrasting reflection of the Aksumite turn to Christianity (Robin 2015, 63). A number of accounts written in Greek, Syriac, Gəʿəz, and Arabic suggest that Jewish communities had existed in the Arabian Peninsula for centuries prior to the emergence of Himyarite Judaism around the turn of the fifth century (Grasso 2023, 72). Although the presence of Jews in

South Arabia would no doubt have played a role in this development if that was indeed the case, the circumstances surrounding the origins of a Jewish mono-theism in Himyar remain veiled by the absence of evidence.

What is clear is that a rather abrupt and radical shift in the religious practices of the South Arabian elite occurs by the end of the fourth century, as indicated by official Himyarite inscriptions, the surviving record of which evinces the utter disappearance of polytheism after c. 380 (Robin 2010, 88). The hundreds of inscriptions in praise of the gods of South Arabia enshrined during the first four centuries CE are subsequently replaced by venerations of monotheistic titles given in unvocalized South Arabian script, such as *'ln* ("God"), *B'l Smyn* ("Lord of Heaven"), and *Rhmnn* ("Merciful"). Furthermore, a number of distinctly Jewish theonyms, such as *B'l Smyn 'lh Ysr['l]* ("Lord of the Sky God of Israel"), are present among surviving Himyarite inscriptions dating to this time period. Taken together with numer-ous other pieces of evidence for the prevalence of Jewish practices in late antique South Arabia (e.g. a seal depicting a menorah), the historical record demonstrates that Himyarite monotheism was heavily influenced by Judaism, if not thoroughly Jewish (Grasso 2023, 74–77).

The Conflicts between Aksum and Himyar

The epigraphic record also illustrates multiple incidents of competitive diplo-matic maneuvers and military conflicts that took place between the Jewish kings of Himyar and their Christian rivals in Aksum. The focus of this section is one such inscription, the surviving fragments of which are catalogued as *RIE* 195, which is commonly known as the Marib inscription. The Marib inscription preserves the conquest in 525 CE of the kingdom of Himyar by the Aksumite king Kaleb, who overthrew the Jewish-Himyarite king Yūsuf As'ar Yath'ar (or Dhū Nuwās). Almost all the surviving sources for the Aksumite invasion of South Arabia in 525 were written by Christians from a confessional perspective. They thus related the narrative in religious terms, casting Kaleb as a dutiful ally of the emperor in Constantinople who invaded Himyar for the sole purpose of rescuing the Christians there from persecution.

According to the majority of the sources, including the *Martyrdom of 'Azqir* and the *Book of the Himyarites* (which is largely based on the more contempor-aneous letter of Simeon of Beth Arsham), the immediate impetus for Kaleb's invasion of Himyar was Yūsuf's persecution of Christians living in South Arabia sometime in the year 523 CE. The texts relate that Christianity had arrived in South Arabia much earlier, around the end of the fifth century (MaAz 1.1; Book of Himyarites II). The evidence suggests that the first converts were made in the city of Najrān, which became the central city for Christians in South Arabia by the sixth century. It was also in the sixth century that the Aksumite king Kaleb carried out his first invasion of South Arabia, in 518 CE, thus resuming the Aksumite control of South Arabia that had come to an end at the close of the third century. After his successful invasion in 518, Kaleb appointed a Christian king named Ma'dīkarib Ya'fur (r. 518–522) as king of Himyar and returned to Aksum. Only four year later, however, the king he appointed as a surrogate ruler died and the Jewish king Yūsuf took his place.

Once he had taken back control in 522, as a number of texts recount, Yūsuf set about consolidating his sovereignty by killing Christians. For example, the *Martyrdom of Arethas* (originally written in Greek c. 560 CE and surviving through its Latin, Gə'əz, and Arabic translations) relates that Yūsuf laid siege to the Christian city of Najrān before killing its inhabitants and burning Christian churches. Yūsuf's attacks set off a chain reaction of events over the next several years, the sum of which not only illustrates the causes underlying the demise of South Arabia's Jewish kingdom but also illuminates the ways in which Aksum and Himyar became embroiled within the wider conflicts between Rome and Persia.

According to the *Martyrdom of Arethas*, Yūsuf sought an alliance with Persia along religious lines, given their mutual opposition to Christian states (i.e. Aksum and Rome). In 524, he sent a letter describing his massacre of Christians to be read at a conference held at Ramla, in which both Byzantine and Persian delegates were present. In response, Justin I (r. 518–527), who was the Byzantine emperor at that time, sent an ambassador to Arabia in order to secure the safety of the remaining Christians at the time. The text also claims that Justin simultaneously sent a letter to Kaleb in Aksum, through the mediation of the patriarch in Alexandria, urging the Aksumite king to attack Himyar since Justin himself was too far away to send his own army. In this way, the *Martyrdom of Arethas* allocates agency for Aksum's invasion of South Arabia in 525 primarily to Justin I, while also suggesting that the motivations for the attack were purely religious.

Given the overly confessional nature of the primary sources, recent studies on the history of Aksum and its relationship with pre-Islamic Arabia have provided useful correctives to the traditional interpretation of Kaleb's military and political career. In particular, they have pointed out that his invasions of South Arabia in 518 and 525 were most likely motivated by economic and political factors, with religious justifications being utilized as pretext for military action and the basis for alliance building (Grasso 2023, 92). They have also highlighted the similarities between Kaleb's political strategies and the imperialist policies of Christian Rome.

These policies are often referred to in the scholarship as "Constantinianism," a term utilized to describe Constantine's paradigmatic use of religion for political ends, a strategy that continued to be practiced by Roman/Byzantine emperors for centuries. One key aspect of Constantinianism involved using the pretext of defending the rights of Christians living in hostile territories as a justification for military attack. For example, Constantine invoked the rescue of Christians living in the eastern Roman Empire when he attacked Licinius in 324 CE in order to become sole ruler of the empire (Barnes 1976). In the same vein, Kaleb utilized the rescue of Christians living in South Arabia as a *casus belli* to legitimize his attack of Himyar in 518, even before Yūsuf's persecution of Christians in 523 (Rukuni 2020, 2).

Several other factors indicate that Kaleb's motivations for his invasion of 525 were not purely religious. The *Christian Topography* of Cosmas Indicopleustes, which is discussed in more detail in Section 1, indicates that it was Kaleb who requested that Cosmas copy the inscription on the Adulis throne in light of his imminent campaign across the Red Sea to invade Himyar (*Top. Chr.* 2.56). Cosmas's account aligns quite well with the timeline for Kaleb's 525 invasion as evidenced by the surviving epigraphic evidence in South Arabia. It also demonstrates that Kaleb was at least in part motivated by the desire to expand Aksum's territories back to its true boundaries as understood by earlier Aksumite kings, who beginning in the third century never ceased to make irredentist claims over South Arabia.

Evidence from South Arabian inscriptions, which were erected by Yūsuf himself, also suggests that Kaleb's invasion of 525 was prompted most immediately by economic concerns. In these inscriptions dating to 523, Yūsuf claims that he killed hundreds of Aksumites who were living in the Himyarite capital of Zhafār, and he also blockaded the harbor of Mandab on the Red Sea coast (Grasso 2023, 96). This action would have effectively severed Aksum's access to Red Sea ports on the Arabian coast, which had been crucial components of its domination of the maritime trade network that extended all the way from India to the Roman provinces along the Mediterranean Sea. The Arabian port cities were particularly critical for the lucrative trade of frankincense, perfumes, and spices, as recounted in several Greek and Latin sources from Herodotus to Pliny the Elder to the *Periplus of the Erythrean Sea* (Casson 1989, 120).

Therefore, regaining control of the valuable commercial centers in South Arabia that he had lost to Yūsuf's attacks was most likely Kaleb's primary motivation for invading Himyar a second time. When he returned to South Arabia in 525 for his second campaign, the attack he launched proved much more fatal to Jewish rule in the region than his first expedition. According to the *Book of the Himyarites*, following his victory over Yūsuf, Kaleb put to death a large number of Jews who refused to convert to Christianity. The *Life of Gregentios* further adds that he remained in South Arabia for three years, where he destroyed Jewish sanctuaries along with the temples of the non-Jewish tribes in the region. In their place, he constructed Christian churches in numerous cities throughout South Arabia. These actions mirror Constantine's patronage of Christians in the eastern Roman Empire after his conquest of Licinius, which served to legitimize his military victories and subsequent rule.

Aksumite Propaganda in South Arabia

In addition, whereas he commemorated his first victory in Himyar by setting up a monument in Aksum, the second time around, in 525, Kaleb erected his victory monument in Marib, a city in the Sabaean region of South Arabia. This Marib inscription is curiously written only in the Classical Ethiopic (or *fidäl*) script, countering the Aksumite custom of composing victory inscriptions in Greek and Gəʿəz, the latter typically written in both the Ethiopic (read left to right) and the Pseudo-Sabaic (read right-to-left) scripts. Its monolingualism notwithstanding, the inscription reveals a number of important themes about how Aksumite rulers sought to portray their place within the broader religious and sociopolitical narratives circulating throughout the late antique world.

The Marib inscription demonstrates Kaleb's strategy for narrativizing the renewed Christian rule he sought to establish in South Arabia, in parallel to how Roman emperors like Constantine portrayed themselves in Christian terms to substantiate their rule. The inscription is interspersed throughout with allusions to and quotations from both the Old and the New Testaments of the Christian Bible.[11] One underlying motif connecting these passages is the idea that the people of God put their trust in him, and he rewards them by raising them up as victors over their enemies. This biblicized framing of Kaleb's conquest over Yūsuf and the Jewish kingdom of Himyar functions to enshrine the Aksumite victory as tangible proof of the belief that Christians had replaced Jews as the true people of the God of the Bible.

Moreover, the Marib inscription also contains another remarkable claim to the heritage of ancient Israel, wherein a direct connection appears to be made between Kaleb and king David. The inscription features a reference to "the glory of David" (*kebra dāwīt*), in a striking parallel to the expansive ethnomyth about the Israelite origins of Ethiopia's royal family that appears in the medieval Ethiopic work the *Glory of the Kings* (*Kebra Negast*). The paucity of evidence

---

[11] For example, lines 20–21 of the inscription draw from Matthew 6.33 and read: "seek first the righteousness ... will be added to you" (*RIE* 195). This line from the Gospels appears side by side with several passages taken from the Psalter, including Psalms 20, 66, and 68.

for the emergence history of the latter occludes any conclusive statements from being made about its relationship to Kaleb's portrayal of himself in the sixth-century Marib inscription (Munro-Hay 2001). However, it is striking that a legendary account of Kaleb's reign is recounted in chapter 117 of the *Glory of the Kings*, in which he is depicted not only as the protector of Christian realms but also as the direct descendant of Solomon through the Queen of Sheba.

Whether or not the claim to the Davidic royal line etched on the Marib monument inspired the subsequent dramatization of that same narrative in medieval Ethiopia, it is clear that both sources share the same strategy of putting the national epic of ancient Israel to use toward propagandist legitimizations of political rule. In the case of Kaleb's inscription, which was deliberately erected in South Arabia as opposed to Aksum, the claim to "the glory of David" may have been promulgated as a response to the claims by the Jewish kings of Himyar that they represented "the People of Israel" (*s 'bn Ysr 'l*), a title attested in several Himyarite inscriptions.

Although written centuries later, the *Glory of the Kings* similarly asserts that Ethiopia's Christians have replaced Israel's Jews as God's chosen people.

The parallels between the two sources might indicate that this distinctively Ethiopian politicization of the biblical saga, characterized by its portrayal of Ethiopian kings as direct descendants of David, may have been circulating as early as the sixth century. It may further indicate that Aksumite kings decisively sought to portray their kingdom in Greco-Roman terms as both Ethiopia and the land of the Queen of Sheba, two toponyms that in some cases were conflated and understood to be references to the same realm.[12] If that was indeed the case, the Marib inscription of 525 may constitute a very early example of an Aksumite ethnomyth that served as actionable discourse for military and political domination over territories on the other side of the Red Sea, which just so happened to be of critical importance for the major imperial powers of the day.

For example, the critical importance of the region for the Byzantine emperors in Constantinople is demonstrated in part by their continuing practice of sending delegates to Aksumite rulers in both South Arabia and Aksum itself. In his *History of the Wars*, Procopius relates that Justinian sought to ally himself with the Ethiopians in order to counteract the Persians and the Arab and Jewish tribes in the Arabian Peninsula who were loyal to them (*Wars* 1.10). With this goal in mind, Justinian sent a Byzantine ambassador named Nonnosus first to Arabia and then to Aksum. Nonnosus was the third generation in a family of Byzantine ambassadors, and the fact that he was sent to both Arabia and Aksum suggests

---

[12] For example, in his *Jewish Antiquities*, Josephus refers to the Queen of Sheba as the queen from Egypt and Ethiopia (*AJ* 8.5.5).

that he was probably able to speak both Arabic and Gǝʿǝz. Nonnosus reached Aksum via Adulis and took copious notes on what he saw in East Africa during his travels and the opulent reception he received from King Kaleb.

Not much is known about Kaleb after his second invasion of Himyar and Nonnosus's visit. The *Ethiopian Synaxarium*, wherein he is celebrated as a saint of the church, reports that, after putting an end to the persecution of Christians in South Arabia, he returned to East Africa. He then abdicated his throne and entered a monastery to live the remainder of his life as a monk. The *Martyrdom of Arethas* relates the same story, adding that, after he took the monastic vow, he sent his royal crown to Jerusalem. These hagiographic accounts of Kaleb's later years remain unverified as there are no surviving mentions of him in any inscriptions or coins after 525. By contrast, his legacy as a protector of Christians lives on in the Ethiopian-Eritrean Orthodox traditions, having been expanded over the centuries in texts like the *Glory of the Kings*. He even becomes a saint in the Catholic tradition in the early modern period as Saint Elesbaan, the Latinized version of his indigenous Gǝʿǝz title, Ǝllä Aṣbǝḥa.

Aksumite Legacies in the Arabian Peninsula

In the aftermath of Kaleb's conquests in South Arabia, Ethiopian kings continued to rule in South Arabia for a few more decades. Similar to the ruler he put in place after his victory in 518, the king Kaleb installed after his defeat of Yūsuf was himself quickly replaced by a more powerful Ethiopian Christian named Abraha. Abraha's origins reveal the close economic and cultural entanglements between the Aksumite and the Byzantine Empires, since he was an Aksumite born in Adulis but his father was a Byzantine merchant who had been working there (Bowersock 2013, 111). After overthrowing the king Kaleb had appointed, Abraha rebelled against Aksum and took control of South Arabia himself. Kaleb launched two military campaigns to bring Abraha's kingdom back into Aksumite control, but both of them failed to accomplish their mission.

Abraha's short-lived successes in consolidating his power as the Christian king of South Arabia can be glimpsed from several of his inscriptions that have survived. One such inscription (also erected in Marib) reports that, like the Jewish king Yūsuf before him, Abraha convened a conference and invited ambassadors from the Byzantine, Persian, and Aksumite Empires. That all of these major powers sent delegates to attend his conference indicates that Abraha's regional government had garnered a level of recognition on the international stage. It also demonstrates just how critical control of the port cities on the Arabian coast was for the economic welfare of the Byzantines, the Persians, and the Aksumites alike.

Another inscription suggests that, in 552 CE, Abraha attempted to further consolidate his power by bringing other regions of the Arabian Peninsula under his control. According to Procopius's *Wars,* the Aksumite rebel king sought to capture territories in central Arabia that were under the influence of Persia (*Wars* 1.20.13). Abraha's campaign to bring the Persian-influenced regions under his control, and thereby strengthen his alliance with the Byzantines and the Aksumites, was ultimately unsuccessful. He left his kingdom to his two sons, named Aksum and Masruq, who successively ruled over South Arabia after the death of their father. Ethiopian rule in South Arabia was brought to an end once and for all when a Jewish king named Sayf ibn dhi Yazan succeeded in driving out the Aksumites with the support of an army sent by the Persian king Chosroes I (Bowersock 2013, 116–117).

In addition to demonstrating Aksum's global entanglements, the stories of the Aksumite rulers who reigned in South Arabia during the sixth century also illustrate the impact that Aksum exerted on the political and cultural world out of which Islam would emerge. The events surrounding the tenures of Kaleb and Abraha as rulers in South Arabia, for example, have left contrasting imprints on the Islamic tradition, since the legacies of the Jewish persecution of Christians and Abraha's military campaigns have been memorialized in radically different ways in the Quran. On the one hand, Sūra 85 (*sūrat al-Burūj*) preserves elements of the persecution of Najrān's Christians through the story of ʿAbdallāh ibn al-Thāmir, who is described as an imam put to death by Yūsuf. This Quranic passage evinces its dependence on Christian hagiographies of the martyrdom of Christians living under Jewish rule in South Arabia. It was ostensibly written as an example of how to remain resilient in the face of persecution, which would have been a powerful lesson for the early Muslim community.

On the other hand, Abraha's abortive campaign to take control of central Arabia may have been the event that earned him his reputation in later Muslim accounts as the would-be conqueror whose attempt to destroy Mecca was thwarted by divine intervention. The story of the army defeated by God as related in Sūra 105 (*sūrat al-fīl,* "The Elephant") is read by later Muslim interpreters (e.g. al-Tabarī) as a reference to Abraha's failed attempt to destroy the Kaʿba in Mecca, despite having a large army and war elephants at his disposal (Bowersock 2013, 115). This event is said to have taken place in "the year of the elephant," traditionally identified in the Islamic tradition as 570 CE, the year of Muhammad's birth. Although the traditional timeline does not align with the epigraphic evidence, it nonetheless sketches a poetic chronology wherein 570 simultaneously serves as the end of Ethiopian-Christian rule in South Arabia and the beginning of the story of Islam.

The Aksumite presence in sixth-century Arabia also contextualizes the presence of key Ethiopian figures in the early history of Islam. Perhaps the most well-known among these is the anonymous *negus* ("king") who provides asylum to the earliest followers of Muhammad after they flee Mecca to escape persecution from the Quraysh (Raven 1988). The story of this community, often referred to as the Sahaba, indicates a certain reputation that Aksumite rulers had garnered on the Arabian Peninsula, as well as the continued relations between Arab tribes and the Aksumites across the Red Sea. Aksum's influence on the region that would give birth to Islam can also be gleaned from the large number of Ethiopic loanwords that survive in Arabic through the Quran, such as *mushaf* ("book"), *tābūt* ("ark"), and *al-hawāriyyūn* ("the apostle") (Jeffery 2007).

In conclusion, the Aksumite adoption of Christianity first made by ʿEzana in the fourth century resulted in Aksum's further entrenchment in a global network of alliances grounded in religious identities. The reign of Kaleb in the sixth century, as well as the aftermaths of his successful invasions of South Arabia, demonstrate the extent to which Aksumite control of the region influenced the geopolitics of the day. Regaining command of both the East African and the Arabian coasts of the Red Sea solidified, albeit only briefly, Aksum's position as one of the most important trading centers in the ancient world. Aksumite presence on the Arabian Peninsula also impelled the Arab-Jewish tribes living there to ally themselves with Persia on the pretext of counteracting the Christians in the region. Persia's alliance with the kingdom of Himyar only deepened Aksum's alliance with Constantinople, turning South Arabia into a proxy war for the major empires of the day. The political vacuum created by their wars on the Arabian Peninsula, as well as the strategies of religious statecraft that they employed, helped shape the world out of which Islam would emerge.

4 Endings and Beginnings: The Ethiopian-Eritrean Highlands in Post-Aksumite Times, Seventh–Tenth Centuries

The "Fall" of Aksum

The exact circumstances and timeline surrounding the end of the Aksumite kingdom remain elusive, but its collapse is indisputable. Current understanding suggests that once-thriving key locations, such as the capital city of Aksum and its primary port Adulis, were largely abandoned or even destroyed in the seventh century. Archaeological excavations in modern-day Tigray indicate a sharp decline in Aksum's population. The city's grand buildings quickly fell into disrepair, with evidence of squatting, looting, and destruction. Abandoned quarries, their large stones partially cut yet never finished, speak of the sudden halt of construction projects (Munro-Hay and Fattovich 2003; Phillipson 2014, 209–11).

Trouble seems to have come from multiple directions by the early 600s CE. Local, regional, and transregional political factors played a role, as did environmental changes and natural disasters. The fate of the coastal city of Adulis appears to have been of pivotal importance. Excavations have revealed its sudden abandonment and the destruction of its harbor. The causes proposed by scholars vary – a fire, a war, an earthquake, a flood. Early excavations in 1906 CE unearthed fused copper objects, burnt logs, ash, and charcoal, hinting at devastating fires (Munro-Hay 1982). This notion was supported by digs in the 1960s: underneath thick layers of ash and charcoal, pots were discovered, abandoned in the middle of preparing a meal. Consequently, archaeologist Francis Anfray observed that the "disappearance of Adulis was brutal" and that catastrophe had struck unexpectedly (Anfray 1974, 753). The exact cause of the blaze remains a mystery, however. Arabic sources mention an assault on the port by Muslim troops in 640 CE, the year Arab armies conquered Egypt. Yet, written accounts of the (attempted) sacking of Adulis in fact diverge greatly, depicting the attack as either a thorough success or a total failure (Yohannes Gebre Selassie 2011, 45).

Recent excavations at the site of old Adulis have added a further layer to the narrative: there seems to have been a catastrophic flood. A significant portion of the ancient city, spanning over forty hectares, was found well-preserved beneath more than two meters of river sediment. This suggests intense and rapid flooding, potentially caused by a dam bursting in the aftermath of an earthquake, which would have instantaneously destroyed the city's harbor (Bortolotto, Cattaneo, and Massa 2021; Massa and Cattaneo 2020; Zazzaro et al. 2015). Given the region's location in the African Rift Valley, an area known for active tectonic plate movements, such a theory is plausible. The sudden and total loss of its primary port would have dealt a devastating blow to Aksum's economy, likely fast-tracking its political breakdown.

However, the decline of the kingdom of Aksum was not solely owed to disasters on the Red Sea coast. Paleoenvironmental studies of the northern highlands show a rapid increase in aridity in the Aksumite hinterland after 500 CE, likely leading to soil degradation and deforestation (Marshall et al. 2009). Such environmental change would have been exacerbated by the overexploitation of resources to fund the realm's military campaigns across the Red Sea in the first half of the sixth century, leading to diminished food production. The financial and the human costs of war undoubtedly played a role, too. Gold deposits were increasingly exhausted, and metal availability sharply declined. According to sixth-century Byzantine historian Procopius, many survivors – particularly slaves – of the Himyar campaign refused to return to the Northeast African highlands.

Seeing that Aksum was a broker state that thrived from its ties with the larger late antique world, we must also view its history against developments in the Eastern

Mediterranean region, the Red Sea, and the Indian Ocean world more broadly (see Figure 1). The Justinianic plague, which began to wreak havoc on Eastern Mediterranean societies by the mid sixth century, is one such factor. Given Aksum's role as a hub for merchants and emissaries from distant lands, including plague-stricken Byzantium, it is likely that the disease found its way to Adulis. While we lack detailed written sources and archaeological studies of local aDNA (ancient DNA), it is probable that this high-mortality disease similarly affected populations in the Ethiopian-Eritrean highlands. In any case, recurrent plague outbreaks in the Eastern Mediterranean during the sixth to eighth centuries significantly hampered overall commercial activity, impacting Aksum's internal and external economy (Yohannes Gebre Selassie 2011).

The regional economic landscape was moreover undergoing significant changes during this period. In 570 CE, the Persians seized control of both Himyar and the Red Sea basin, disadvantaging Byzantium and Aksum. Eighty years later, the Arab conquests dramatically reconfigured power dynamics and trade routes from North Africa to Central Asia. Viewed from a Northeast African highland perspective, the major cities of the Levant and the Eastern Mediterranean had initially retained their significance. However, in 762 CE, the Abbasids established a new capital in Baghdad, located significantly farther east. This political transition eventually shifted Mediterranean trade with China in favor of a competing path, creating a preference for a route through the Persian Gulf rather than the Red Sea (Power 2009).

Written and epigraphic sources on the kingdom become exceedingly rare by the mid-seventh century. The minting of coins ceased, as did the construction of monumental buildings, churches, and commemorative stelae (Fattovich 2014). Aksum and particularly its Christian king, the *nagāśī*, feature prominently in early Arabic writing – after all, the Prophet Muhammad had urged his first followers to seek refuge there from persecution in the Arabian Peninsula in 615 CE. Yet, these records are often of a rhetorical or allegorical nature (Raven 1988). They tell us little about the actual realm in the immediate post-Aksumite era. Archaeological and architectural sources meanwhile show that predominantly agricultural Christian communities must have endured on the eastern fringes of the former kingdom, in the vicinity of a trade route that connected the highland interior with the Red Sea coast.[13] Over a stretch of more than 200 miles, small churches were built or carved

---

[13] Today, this trade route is still visible in the form of the northern section of the modern-day Ethiopian A2 motorway and its B20 and Eritrean extensions past Adigrat, which connect the Eastern Ethiopian highland plateau with Eritrea's capital Asmara. The post-Aksumite churches (or their remains, rebuilt over time) have been partially surveyed and reach from Lake Hashenge or Ašange in the south of Tigray to Senafe or Šəmäzana in Eritrea (Lepage 2006; Lepage and Mercier 2005).

Figure 1 Trade routes connecting Afro-Eurasia in the "Medieval Millennium."

Source: © Map by Verena Krebs and Honza Brandeis 2024.

from the living rock between the eighth and the eleventh centuries (Derat 2020a, 34–35; Muehlbauer 2023b, 42–52).

"Silk Road," North African, and Nubian Connections

Given the complex and limited nature of the available material evidence, our ability to speak on the region's history during this period is highly constrained. A good example is the mid-twentieth-century discovery of numerous ancient gold and silver coins at the remote monastery of Däbrä Damo in present-day Tigray. Situated near the old trade route where Christianity persisted, this monastery is perched on a nearly inaccessible mountain. Tradition holds that Zämika᾽el Arägawi, a pivotal figure in the late antique spread of Christianity across the northern Ethiopian-Eritrean highlands, established it. Däbrä Dammo's foundation is thought to have been facilitated by King Gäbrä Mäsqäl, the son of King Kaleb, renowned for leading the sixth-century invasion of Himyar. A significant Christian center already in Aksumite times, it continues to function as a monastery to the present day (Tsegay Berhe Gebre Libanos 2005).

Several hoards of coins were discovered at Däbrä Damo in 1939 and 1940. Among them were over 100 third-century Kushan coins, originating from modern-day India, Pakistan, and Afghanistan, intriguing evidence of Aksum's contacts with the "silk road" in late antiquity.[14] Also found were a great number of gold and silver coins struck in Egypt and North Africa between the seventh and the ninth centuries. Washed out of the topsoil of the *amba*, the tabletop mountain on which the monastery stands, they were embossed with the names of Umayyad and Abbasid caliphs. Today, most are no longer accessible to researchers. They have been sold off or melted down for local monastic use, forcing scholars to rely on the records of a former Italian colonial administrator who documented their "discovery" for academe (Fauvelle 2018, 94–99; Matthews and Mordini 1959; Mordini 1960). A near-total lack of archaeological context restricts our ability to speculate about their journey to the Ethiopian-Eritrean highlands. We know the exact date when and the place where these coins were minted, but they could have arrived in the highlands shortly after their creation or centuries later. Either way, these finds underscore the historical significance of Däbrä Damo as a Christian stronghold – and provide a tantalizing glimpse of the region's connections to the wider world in an era we otherwise still struggle to reconstruct.

What else can then be said about "Ethiopia" in the world of Afro-Eurasia between the late seventh and the ninth centuries? Historians primarily rely on

---

[14] For mentions of "Ethiopia" in Armenian sources and possible contacts between the two regions in the first millennium, also see Pogossian 2021.

external written sources from Egypt and Nubia, which offer some information on what appear to be several different political entities in the region. However, the vast geographical – and sometimes temporal – distance between these writings and the places and times they describe necessitates a particularly critical approach when interpreting these texts. A case in point is an episode from the "History of the Patriarchs," an invaluable source for Christian and Muslim history in Northeast Africa in the later medieval period. This extensive collection of biographies, compiled in Northern Egypt from the eleventh century onwards in Arabic, details the lives of the patriarchs who succeeded to the see of Saint Mark in Alexandria. One passage, presumably drawing from older Coptic works, reports on events from the late seventh century. At first glance, it seems to speak about a strained relationship between the Christians of Nubia (*al-Nūba*) and the Christians of what are now the highlands of Ethiopia and Eritrea (*al-Ḥabaša*).

Throughout the Middle Ages, modern-day Sudan and the Ethiopian-Eritrean plateau were home to sovereign Christian kingdoms. The different realms all followed the miaphysite doctrine – a belief within Christianity maintaining that Christ has one single nature that is both divine and human – and relied on the Patriarch of Alexandria in Egypt for ecclesiastical leadership. The latter explains why their affairs are regularly mentioned in the "History." Yet, upon closer inspection, the episode described there does not concern the political entity of *al-Ḥabaša* (an Arabic term commonly used to describe the Christian areas of Ethiopia and Eritrea) at all. Instead, the "History" here tells of a political conflict between the two Nubian kingdoms of Makuria and Nobatia, which – alongside Alodia – were successors to the ancient Nubian kingdom of Meroe. By 707 CE, Makuria had forcefully annexed the formerly independent Nobatia (Munro-Hay 1997, 111). Writing centuries after the event in Egypt, the compilers of the "History" seem to have confused the different Christian realms to the south. The passage, however evocative it might appear at first glance, thus offers no insight into the history of the post-Aksumite Ethiopian-Eritrean highlands at the turn of the eighth century.

Beyond such historiographical mix-ups, fragmentary epigraphic evidence from a later date hints at intriguing links between Nubia and the northern Ethiopian-Eritrean highlands. One connection may be seen in the monumental ninth-century inscriptions unearthed in Faras, the former capital of Nobatia and seat of the *eparch* or bishop in Makurian times. These inscriptions reveal the local usage of four different dating systems, one of which is "Ethiopian" (Munro-Hay 1997, 122). Another comes in the form of a roughly coeval memorial, once placed in the façade of the old St. Mary's church in the village of Ham in modern-day Eritrea. It, too, indicates contacts between Christians in the highlands and the Nubian kingdoms during this period. It is a funerary inscription, written in Gəʿəz, and commemorates "Giḥo, the daughter of Mängäša," stating that she died just before Christmas. Rich in scripture quotations that allude to biblical exegesis, the text consists of fifty-four words in fifteen lines, carefully carved into a large stone tablet. Scholars have noted that the tablet is shaped like a Meroitic offering table and bears other stylistic similarities to inscriptions found in Meroe and Alodia – and thus pre-Christian and Christian Nubia (Bausi 2021; Kropp 1999).

Owed to unconventional numerical signs, the year of Giḥo's death remains a subject of debate. Manfred Kropp interpreted the numerals as Nubian figures and proposed a date of 873 CE (Kropp 1999, 169). In contrast, Alessandro Bausi read them as adapted Greek numbers, suggesting that Giḥo passed away in 974 CE (Bausi 2021, 3). Regardless of the precise date, the funerary inscription from Ham indicates a lasting Christian presence in the southern Eritrean highlands in a period of scarce local written records.

Today, Ham is a secluded village near the renowned monastery of Däbrä Libanos, just a short distance from the modern Ethiopian-Eritrean border. It lies on the same ancient trade route where small churches from the post-Aksumite period dotted the landscape in the eighth and ninth centuries. Notably, it appears that the area's Christian communities maintained connections with the broader Greek-speaking Christian world, especially the Nubian Christian world, in a period often characterized as a "dark age." Giḥo's memorial, together with the inscriptions from Nubia, hints at the role of the Greek language in these contacts. Greek had a long tradition in both regions: as the language of the New Testament and late antique Egypt, it was one of the languages used in the Nubian kingdoms alongside Coptic, Old Nubian, and Arabic. Similarly, Greek had been one of the languages of Aksum, and the gospels were translated from Greek into Gəʿəz in Aksumite times. The language may thus have served as a communicative bridge between these two distinct African Christian spheres.[15] However, our observations and interpretations must remain tentative for now. Scholarship on both Nubia and Ethiopia has long been fragmented along linguistic lines and national borders, and a comprehensive study of Nubian–Ethiopian interaction and exchange still largely remains a desideratum.

---

[15] Indeed, a particular linguistic feature and formulation found in a twelfth-century land grant of Zagʷe king Ṭänṭäwədəm has led Alessandro Bausi to propose that administrative practices of Greco-Mediterranean origin were present in Ethiopia at this time. Specifically, Bausi suggests that Byzantine notarial customs, similarly employed by Greek scribes in Norman Sicily, may also have made their way to the Ethiopian-Eritrean highlands (Bausi 2023).

Nubian, Egyptian, and Yemenite Connections

Fragmentary evidence also hints at remarkably close relations between Christians in the Ethiopian-Eritrean highlands and the Nubian kingdoms in the tenth century. It, again, comes to us from the "History of the Patriarchs," which specifically recounts an exchange that took place during the patriarchate of Philotheos, who presided over the See of Alexandria from 979 to 1003 CE. Sometime in the last quarter of the tenth century, a nameless Christian sovereign from "Ethiopia" dispatched a letter to King Jirgis II of Makuria, who had ruled the Nubian kingdom from 969 CE. King Jirgis II, in turn, sent an embassy carrying the original missive as well as his own letter to Patriarch Philotheos in Egypt, where a version of the exchange would subsequently be copied into the "History" (Munro-Hay 1997, 133–34).

According to this source, a Christian king from the Ethiopian-Eritrean highlands (*al-Ḥabaša*) sought aid from the Nubian king after a calamitous war. The conflict, waged by a queen of the *Banū l-Ham(u)wīya*, had devastated his realm: cities were burnt, and churches destroyed. The queen had also taken many captives and made the unnamed Christian ruler a fugitive in his kingdom. The chronicler of the "History" suggests that this catastrophe was perceived as divine retribution for transgressions committed by the king's father against the Church and God. The specifics of these offenses remain unclear. Yet, with its local clergy dead and its churches in ruins, the kingdom of *al-Ḥabaša* teetered on the brink of political and spiritual extinction. Rebuilding the churches and consecrating new clergy were contingent on the Patriarch of Alexandria appointing a new metropolitan to guide the local flock. Consequently, this otherwise unidentified "Ethiopian" monarch implored the Makurian king Jirgis II to pen a letter to the patriarch in Egypt, supporting his request of the patriarch's forgiveness, prayers, and assistance. In response, Jirgis II dispatched letters and messengers to Patriarch Philotheus, who acceded to the plea. According to the passage in the "History," a monk named Daniel was then sent from a prominent Egyptian monastery to the highlands, where his arrival was greeted "with joy, and God removed from them His wrath and put an end to the affair with the woman who had risen against them" (Sāwīris ibn al-Muqaffaʿ 1948, 171–72).

Despite its brevity, this episode implies a remarkable depth of familiarity and trust between these two very different Christian kings in Northeast Africa in the tenth century. The political organization of "Ethiopia" during this period remains largely obscure, preventing even an educated guess at the name of our highland sovereign. By contrast, King Jirgis II of Makuria is attested as a well-established statesman in several contemporaneous sources from both

Nubia and Egypt. He had recently rebuffed intimidation efforts by the Fatimids, a Maghribi Shīʿite dynasty that conquered Egypt and established its new capital of Cairo in 969 CE. Within a few years, Fatimid emissaries were sent south to renew the *baqṭ* (بقط), an ancient treaty that had bound Egypt and Nubia together since the first Arab conquests. In the face of considerable pressure to convert to Islam, Jirgis II firmly declined – and, in fact, invited the Fatimid ambassador to embrace Christianity instead (Fauvelle 2018, 39–41). It is thus not surprising that an unnamed king from the embattled Ethiopian-Eritrean highlands would seek the support of his Christian neighbor farther up the Nile to help relay a desperate request to the ecclesiastical leadership in Egypt. Makuria had, after all, successfully demonstrated its resilience as a bastion of Christianity, its king able to hold his ground against the new rulers of Egypt, while still maintaining its dependence on the patriarchate in Alexandria.

A key element of the above episode from the "History" is corroborated in contemporaneous Arabic sources: they also state that a non-Christian queen took control of large parts of the Ethiopian-Eritrean highland plateau in the second half of the tenth century. In his most famous work, the *Ṣūrat al-arḍ*, written in the 980s, Arab traveler and writer Ibn Ḥawqal reports that the "country of al-Ḥabaša (الحبشي) has been ruled by a woman for a number of years." He notes that she had killed its Christian king, known as the *Ḥaḍānī* (حضاني), and claimed his realm. This expanded her territory into a vast, limitless country without well-defined borders, encompassing both her original king-dom – thought to be to the south – and the *Ḥaḍānī*'s domain. It stretched from the deep interior to the deserts on each side of the highlands and the Red Sea (Ibn Ḥawqal 1964, 56). Although Ibn Ḥawqal does not reveal the queen's religion or precise origin, he emphasizes her long reign, spanning roughly thirty years, and the size of her dominion. According to him, intriguing reports about her had reached Egypt, and she enjoyed active, friendly relations with the Ziyādīs of Yemen, a powerful dynasty within the Arabian Peninsula at the time (Andersen 2000, 32–33).

Another Arabic source, penned by an anonymous tenth-century author in Egypt, also makes mention of the queen's reign, substantiating Ibn Ḥawqal's account. In a description of an embassy sent by the Yemenite ruler Isḥāq ibn Ziyād to a principality in what is now Iraq in 969/970 CE, the text offhandedly notes that Isḥāq's diplomatic gift – a zebra – had originally been sent as a present from the lands of *al-Ḥabaša*, "over which a woman reigns" (el-Chennafi 1976, 120).

This source distinctly situates the tenure of our unnamed non-Christian "Ethiopian" queen in time, confirming that she held power by 970 CE. Furthermore, we know that Ibn Ḥawqal had gathered his information on Christian Northeast Africa during an extended stay in Egypt in the 950s and completed his work on the *Ṣūrat* around 988 CE (Derat 2020a, 36). As such, we can reasonably deduce that the queen's rule falls squarely into the second half of the tenth century. By the late 960s CE, she had consolidated and established her authority enough to maintain diplomatic relations with other sovereigns in the Red Sea basin, particularly in Yemen. Meanwhile, the events detailed in the "History" suggest that she reigned over the highlands until at least the early 980s, when Philotheos was Patriarch of Alexandria. Both would corroborate Ibn Ḥawqal's claim of a decades-long rule, if not a full thirty years.

Late medieval Gəʿəz sources also refer to the episode. A section in the Ethiopian Sənkəssar or "Synaxary," a hagiographic work commemorating saints, martyrs, and events from the late fourteenth century, is based mainly on the above story from the "History of the Patriarchs." An entry for Philotheos, the Patriarch of Alexandria, to be read on the 12th of Ḥədar (November 21), quotes a version of the letter sent by the unnamed "Ethiopian" king to King Jirgis II of Makuria in the last quarter of the tenth century. The Sənkəssar omits any mention of a queen, however. It simply speaks of "enemies" who had revolted against the Christian king, taken captives, burnt cities, and plundered the churches (Budge 1928, 233–34).

Interestingly, other medieval chronicles and local apocryphal folk history – undoubtedly drawing on the "History of the Patriarchs" – tend to focus on a non-Christian female ruler as a harbinger of destruction at the turn of the millennium. She is traditionally known as "Gudit" or "Judith" or simply as "Ǝsato" – "the fire," responsible for devastating churches and palaces, particularly in the old capital of Aksum. Many legends explicitly style her as a Jewish queen: the prevailing narrative depicts this figure as a disgraced Aksumite Christian woman, possibly from the royal family, forced to flee the country after experiencing humiliation and physical harm at the hands of a local priest. Some stories even narrate that she was forced into prostitution. Subsequently, she met and married a Jewish king – possibly an allusion to late antique Himyar – whom she persuaded to exact revenge on Aksum for the degradation she had endured. Here, Gudit is conceived as a counternarrative to the Queen of Sheba, to whose son by the biblical king Solomon the Solomonic rulers of the late Middle Ages would trace their ancestry. Indeed, fifteenth-century Gəʿəz sources specify that no woman should ever hold the throne of the Christian kingdom. Gudit, we may assume, became a cautionary tale that embodied the dangers of such a rule (Dege-Müller 2018, 271).[16]

---

[16] Fascinatingly, subsequent Gəʿəz chronicles endeavored to incorporate this enigmatic figure into a larger Christian conceptualization of "Ethiopia." They elevated Gudit to royal status, portraying her as a wronged king's granddaughter, and characterized her as either a pagan or a willing convert to Judaism. This depiction seemingly alludes to the alleged Israelite origins of the Zagʷe dynasty ruling from the eleventh century to 1270 CE, and legitimized a core principle

It is important to acknowledge our current inability to determine the identity of this long-ruling queen of the *Banū l-Ham(u)wīya* with any certainty.[17] All attempts to locate her must remain unverifiable hypotheses for now. Yet, we also know this: at the turn of the millennium, several powerful, centralized polities that left no written records thrived in the more southerly highlands of what is now Ethiopia. Among them was the Shay Culture, which erected hundreds of magnificent megaliths in Šäwa and Amhara from the ninth century onwards, and is known to have been connected to a wider Islamic and Indian Ocean world by the 1200s (Alebachew Belay Birru 2020a, 2020b; Fauvelle 2020; Fauvelle and Poissonnier 2012).

While the funerary inscription for Giḥo, the beloved daughter of Mängäša, and the scattered churches along the trade route from southern Tigray to Eritrea bear witness to the enduring presence of Christianity in the northern regions, our understanding of the post-Aksumite political landscape remains hazy. Arab chroniclers of the eighth and ninth centuries, such as al-Yaʿqūbī and al-Masʿūdī, continued to depict the dominions of the *najāshī* (another term for the Christian king of *al-Ḥabaša*, referring to Aksum and its successors) as a powerful and *Christian* stronghold well into the mid tenth century – precisely when our non-Christian queen assumed power, steering the realm toward Yemen and the Muslim world (Munro-Hay 1997, 122). But did these authors write about the Northeast African highlands – or were they, again, actually referring to the Nubian kingdoms farther up the Nile? Depending on the timeline we accept, the death of Giḥo shortly before the Christmas of either 873 or 974 CE would have immediately preceded or coincided with a period of tremendous social and political upheaval.

An intriguing glimpse into this era comes from another epigraphic source, indicating civil unrest and war. Sometime between the ninth and the twelfth centuries, a certain *ḥaṣani* Danəʾel, son of Däbrä Fərem (or Däbrä Afrem), appropriated an old Aksumite throne base and had it adorned with several

---

of the *Kəbrä nägäśt*, which asserted that no woman should ever ascend to the throne of "Ityop̣ya" or "Ethiopia" during Solomonic times (after 1270 CE). Such a narrative reflects both an awareness of the highland territories' inherent diversity and a perceived necessity to unite them under universal Christian hegemony based on a mythology of biblical descent.

[17] Several hypotheses have been proposed by scholars regarding her origins. *Banū*, in Arabic, refers to a specific clan within an ethnic group. For instance, the Prophet Muhammad belonged to the Banū Hāšim clan of the Qurayš tribe. In the case of this queen, her name – *Ham(u)wīya* – is open to interpretation. Some scholars suggest that it is an Arabicized version of *al-Damūtah*, indicating Damot in modern-day Šäwa, a southern kingdom known for practicing local indigenous beliefs until the thirteenth century. Other interpretations read the term as referring to *al-Yahūdīya*, suggesting that she was "the Jewish queen," or *al-Haghouīya*, the "queen of the Agaws." There are also suggestions that she might have been a Sidaama queen of the Bali Sultanate, one of the southernmost territories mentioned by name in later medieval Gəʿəz sources (Derat 2018, 107, 241).

roughly carved Gəʿəz inscriptions. These narrate his subjugation of rival "tribes" or "peoples" and his conflict with another individual – the *ḥaṣani* Karuray. Danəʾel recounts defending the city of Aksum against a rival group, the "Wälqayt people," after they had plundered a third group, the "Barya." He asserts that he dethroned the "king of Aksum" and ended his reign after that ruler attempted to annex his lands. In the wake of his defeat at the hands of Danəʾel, the deposed opponent was captured and made a tributary. At least, this is the narrative according to the victor, who etched his version of history in stone for posterity (Munro-Hay and Nosnitsin 2005; Yohannes Gebre Selassie 2011, 43–44).

Much about Danəʾel remains shrouded in mystery. His Christian name is evident, and the title he employs – *ḥaṣani* – aligns with the Arabic term that Ibn Ḥawqal used in his tenth-century source to refer to the king of Aksum.[18] We know virtually nothing about his rival, Karuray, though it is worth noting that Danəʾel accords him the same title. Danəʾel's inscription thus memorializes the triumph of one Christian leader over another in a fragmented political landscape, where multiple groups – several seemingly Christian – vied for dominance. The decision to repurpose a late antique throne base within the former Aksumite capital suggests that Danəʾel's adversaries shared his faith. It furthermore implies that inscribing oneself into the stones of the city retained symbolic importance – indicating that even after decades, possibly centuries, of decline and abandonment, the old capital of Aksum still bore the power to "make kings" (Fauvelle 2018, 90–93).

Against such a tumultuous and volatile backdrop, the decades-long reign of a non-Christian queen becomes both more intriguing and more intelligible. Amid the chaos of petty rivalries and pervasive raiding among different groups centered on a *ḥaṣani*, she seemingly managed to consolidate the remnants of the post-Aksumite Christian territories into her already existent kingdom – a feat that the various *ḥaṣani* had failed to accomplish or maintain. Nonetheless, by the 980s, a Christian faction seems to have regained a degree of independent sovereignty. Its power was sufficiently established to organize a diplomatic mission to King Jirgis II of Makuria – and fragile enough to necessitate his intercession with the Coptic patriarchate. As Marie-Laure Derat has noted, Alexandria had repeatedly refused to appoint bishops to the Horn of Africa throughout the tenth century. Yet, a metropolitan was necessary to initiate the rebuilding processes that would ensure the reestablishment of Christian authority in the region (Derat 2018, 107–8).

---

[18] While *ḥaṣani* literally translates as "tutor," "nurse," or "guardian" (of children), it appears to have signified a leadership role during this period, denoting perhaps a governor or warlord.

In the decades thereafter, Christianity in the Ethiopian-Eritrean highlands experienced a resurgence. This revival was undoubtedly a response to the impassioned appeal made by Alexandria's more southerly Christian dependents in the last quarter of the tenth century. It also seems to have been influenced by the strategic interests of the new Muslim rulers of Egypt – the Fatimids, who had assumed power just years before the unnamed Ethiopian king sought the assistance of Jirgis II. The Fatimids, for their part, pursued their own religious and economic policies toward the Horn of Africa. As we shall see in Section 5, both Christian and Muslim groups in the highlands would soon begin to flourish on a scale not seen for centuries.

5 Cosmopolitan Communities: Fatimid Red Sea Trade and the Horn of Africa, Tenth–Twelfth Centuries

Fatimid Trading Settlements and Sovereign Muslim Communities

The Fatimid Caliphate – initially based in *Ifrīqiyā* (modern-day Tunisia and Algeria) – seized control of Egypt in 969 CE. Within a span of just a few years, the Fatimids established a new capital, Cairo (*al-Qāhira*), at the site of an earlier Rashidun city, Fustat (*al-Fusṭāṭ*). Straddling the Nile and perched at the edge of its Delta, the city was ideally situated for command over important Mediterranean, Red Sea, and Indian Ocean trade routes. This strategic location allowed Egypt's new rulers to dominate commerce and extend their influence across the larger region, seeding trading colonies along the way. The coastal territories of the Horn of Africa that fringed the Ethiopian-Eritrean highland plateau – including the straits of Bab-el-Mandeb, a chokepoint within this network – were no exception. Recent research indicates the existence of several Fatimid-aligned settlements both on the coast of modern-day Eritrea and in the northern Ethiopian highlands by the late tenth century.

For decades, trade routes in the Persian Gulf had overshadowed those of the Red Sea. However, a series of interconnected developments began to tilt the scales back in favor of Egypt and the Red Sea in the 900s CE. These included significant geopolitical shifts within the Muslim realms of the extended Mediterranean, including the Fatimid conquest of Northeast Africa. Economic factors also played a crucial role: there was a mining boom in gold and silver in Sudan and Yemen, and flax cultivation surged in Egypt – a development that fueled mills from Tunisia to Sicily. Moreover, spurred by demand from mining and farming activities and the deployment of slave soldiers (*mamlūks*) to fortify Red Sea emirates, the slave trade expanded significantly. Written sources document the regional emergence of several distinct and influential mercantile classes of different religions. According to Timothy Power, the Red Sea trade resurgence reached its apex during the first hundred years of Fatimid rule in Egypt – and thus the late tenth and eleventh centuries (Power 2009).

The Dahlak Archipelago

Within this larger network, the Dahlak archipelago – a group of over 100 arid islands located just off the Eritrean coast in the Red Sea – soon emerged as a pivotal communication and trading hub. At the intersection of long-distance and interregional routes, the islands connected the Eritrean coast and its hinterland with the extended Red Sea region: Egypt, the Arabian Peninsula, and the Persian Gulf. Here, luxury items from the Indian Ocean were traded alongside goods from the Ethiopian-Eritrean plateau – foodstuffs, ivory, animal skins, fragrant woods, and perfume ingredients, as well as enslaved individuals (Insoll 2001).

By the tenth century, Dahlak was under Muslim control. Initially seized during the early Arab conquests, the islands garnered notoriety as a penal settlement in Umayyad and Abbasid times, infamous for their punishing cycles of brutally hot winds and torrential rains. Control over these harsh yet strategically critical isles – where all water had to be imported or sourced from cisterns due to a lack of freshwater – subsequently alternated between Christian "Ethiopian" and Muslim Yemenite dynasties, according to Arabic sources. The archipelago's inhabitants, meanwhile, had long been Muslim. By the late 900s CE, the archaeological and written record indicates the emergence of a local sovereign sultanate at Dahlak. It was aligned with the Ziyādīs in Yemen and the Fatimid Caliphate in Egypt (Lusini 2002, 247).[19]

This sultanate, established on Dahlak al-Kabīr – the largest island in the archipelago – persevered for over three centuries. Hundreds of finely crafted funerary stelae, carved from valuable black basalt, bear witness to the community's prosperity and cosmopolitanism, as well as to its adherence to Ismāʿīlī Islam, the Shīʿite doctrine of the Fatimid Caliphate (Muehlbauer 2021, 10). Most stelae, dating between the ninth and the eleventh centuries, feature inscriptions in Naskhi and Kufic script. Their *nisbas* – attributive names indicating a family's geographic origin – suggest a trading community with wide-reaching connections that spanned from the Caucasus and Persia to the Iberian peninsula (Schneider 1983).

The inscriptions on the stelae suggest that the coastal community's ties extended not just to Western Europe and Central Asia; they also stretched

---

[19] In fact, a sovereign ruler (*sayyid*) and subsequently a sultan (*sulṭān*) – drawn from the Naǧāḥids, a dynasty of Ethiopian slaves who had ruled in Yemen in the early 1000s CE – are firmly attested as ruling Dahlak by the eleventh century. Stelae in Dahlak and Qūṣ, an important mercantile center in Upper Egypt, evidence the close contacts of merchants from these two trading hubs (Chekroun and Hirsch 2020b, 90).

toward the Eritrean hinterland, to Muslim settlements deep within the Ethiopian highland plateau. Recent archaeological findings have shed new light on one such inland locality, rewriting the early history of Islam in Ethiopia and Eritrea (Loiseau 2020b; Loiseau et al. 2021). It appears that the residents of Bilet, near the modern-day village of Kʷiḥa in Tigray, maintained active contacts and direct relations with both the Dahlak Sultanate and the Fatimid Caliphate in Egypt between the tenth and the thirteenth centuries. As we shall see at the end of this section, these communities' trading activities also had a considerable impact on their Christian neighbors in the kingdoms ruled by the so-called *ḥaṣani* (a Gəʿəz term denoting petty kings, chieftains, or even generals in contemporary usage).

Highland Communities in Eastern Tigray

As mentioned in Section 4 (see the section "The 'Fall' of Aksum"), Muslim tradition posits an early introduction of Islam to the region. Arabic narratives recount how Muhammad's first followers, seeking refuge from persecution in Mecca, established a settlement in the seventh-century Aksumite highlands even before the *hiğra*, the Prophet's migration to Medina in 622 CE (Chekroun and Hirsch 2020b, 88). Yet, archaeological sources indicating a Muslim presence beyond the Red Sea coast and within the highland interior long remained elusive. Concrete evidence has been uncovered only recently: here, systematic surveys and preliminary excavations revealed the presence of thriving Islamic communities in what is now Eastern Tigray, northern Ethiopia, dating back to the 970s CE (Loiseau 2020b; Loiseau et al. 2021).[20]

In 2018, the first systematic archaeological campaign at Bilet near Kʷiḥa, just a short distance from the Tigrayan regional capital of Mekelle, immediately doubled the known count of local Muslim funerary stelae to nearly fifty. Alongside the necropolis of the Dahlak archipelago, these stelae form the most significant repository of Arabic inscriptions from the Horn of Africa around the turn of the first millennium. Given that such markers were typically reserved for influential families and wealthy individuals, and considering that the site has been heavily farmed, rebuilt, and even excavated in a gold hunt by later inhabitants, the number of stones documented thus far points to a once sizable population. Most funerary stelae bear Arabic inscriptions in Kufic, the earliest form of Arabic script.

---

[20] Accounts from nineteenth-century European travelers mentioned several funerary stelae inscribed with Arabic writing in this region. Yet, these monuments merely hinted at a past Muslim presence in an area now predominantly inhabited by Orthodox Christians. All inscribed stones had been moved from their original locations, with several even preserved in Christian churches. Thus, mid-twentieth-century scholars could offer only tentative assessments of their historical significance, and speculate on their implications within the wider regional context (Conti Rossini 1937; Schneider 1967).

They indicate a continuous period of habitation from the late tenth to the mid thirteenth centuries (Loiseau 2020b; Loiseau et al. 2021).

The nature and orientation of the burials, as well as the inscriptions, demonstrate the community's deep knowledge of the Quran and Hiǧra calendar, and their adherence to (or, at least, sympathies for) Ismāʿīlīsm, the branch of Shīʿism favored and actively propagated by the Fatimid Caliphate. The stones also anchor the site to a broader Islamic world: the names on the funerary markers in Bilet evoke local, regional, and distant – spiritual and/or ancestral – connections, referencing the Arabian Peninsula, Upper Egypt, and even Fārs in Western Iran (compare Figure 2). Names with uncertain readings, with too many consonants to be of Arabic origin, indicate that the community consisted of local and foreign Muslims (Loiseau et al. 2021, 524–25). The earliest stone, belonging to a certain Ḥafṣ b. ʿUmar al-Yamāmī, dates to the year 972. The last known stele is dated to 1261 CE. Epigraphic and archaeological data suggest a peak period between 1030 and 1080 CE when inscriptions allow us to trace entire families over several generations.

Scholars have long hypothesized about connections between the Dahlak islands and Bilet (Fauvelle-Aymar and Hirsch 2004; Lusini 2002; Schneider 1967). The 2018 excavations uncovered stones that showcase a direct link between the two Muslim communities by the late tenth century: Ḥasnā, the daughter of Ḥafṣ b. ʿUmar al-Yamāmī – whose 972 CE stelae is the oldest

Figure 2 Basalt funerary stele with Arabic writing commemorating the death of of Abū Muḥammad Ǧaʿfar al-Fārisī on February 18, 1040 CE. His *nisba* indicates a connection to Fārs or "Persia."
Source: © Photo by Julien Loiseau and Simon Dorso 2018.

known from Bilet – was buried in the cemetery of Dahlak al-Kabīr in 980 CE. Meanwhile, three of her kinswomen and her father found their final resting place in the mountains of Tigray – some 6,500 feet above sea level and approximately 200 miles inland from her grave on a Red Sea island (Loiseau 2020b, 78; Loiseau et al. 2021, 525). Intriguingly, the lives of this far-flung family coincide with the tumultuous period when the queen of the *Banū l-Ham(u)wīya* had seized power in the Ethiopian-Eritrean highlands. It wasn't until the 980s, shortly after Ḥasnā's death, that the unnamed Christian king mentioned in Section 4 (see the section "Nubian, Egyptian, and Yemenite Connections") sought assistance from King Jirgis II of Markuria in requesting a new metropolitan from Egypt and ultimately reestablished Christian control over parts of the region.

Moreover, recent discoveries suggest that Bilet was not the only thriving Muslim highland community from this period onwards. Approximately twenty miles to the south, at Arra and its surrounding areas, another forty-five funerary stelae provisionally dated to the twelfth and thirteenth centuries were documented only as recently as 2019 (Loiseau 2020b, 93; Loiseau et al. 2021, 510). While the more northerly locality of Wägǝr Ḥariba remains largely unstudied, Wolbert Smidt considers it to have been Tigray's most significant medieval Islamic settlement (Smidt 2010). Many of the above findings remain preliminary so far. Nonetheless, they indicate that the history of early Ethiopian-Eritrean Muslim communities, and their interactions with their Christian environment, will need to be significantly revised in the coming years.

For now, we may observe that these Islamic highland settlements were located on strategic node points. Bilet, Arra, and Wägǝr Ḥariba, like the post-Aksumite churches discussed in Section 4 (see the section "Nubian, Egyptian, and Yemenite Connections"), are situated on the same eastern highland route that saw precious wares – ivory, wood, gold, and the enslaved – transported from the Ethiopian interior to the Eritrean coast.[21] A little to the west, ancient caravan routes linked the salt plains of the Danakil, located at or below sea level, with the Tigrayan highlands (Woldekiros 2019). The notoriously difficult but highly profitable journey, which necessitated a climb of more than 7,000 feet in altitude over just a few miles, took just roughly two weeks to complete (Lusini 2002). It is thus no wonder that Bilet dates back even further in time: preliminary excavations also indicate that it was a notable settlement in Aksumite times. Today, the ruins of a monumental, three-aisled building made out of large, finely hewn limestone blocks are located just a short distance away from both the

---

[21] In fact, when the first European embassy trekked southwards from the Eritrean coast in the early sixteenth century, hoping to reach the court of King Lǝbnä Dǝngǝl in the modern-day region of Amhara, the group crossed through Bilet (Breton and Aytenew Ayele 2019).

medieval Muslim cemetery and the modern-day church of Kʷiḥa Qirqos or Č̣ərqos (Breton and Aytenew Ayele 2019). Bilet's early Muslim inhabitants had settled at a site of some historical importance – at the nexus of not one but several trade routes.

We can also say that the "Seal of Solomon," a hexagram seen as a protective talisman in medieval Islamic culture, is prominently displayed on several funerary markers in Bilet and other Ethiopian sites. While not exclusive to the region, this symbol was seemingly particularly popular among medieval Muslims in the highlands. It is plausible that it served as a recognizable and meaningful sign of a shared Abrahamic faith to the community's Christian neighbors. The motif still adorns protective scrolls, prayer staffs, and other liturgical furnishings today. One of the funerary stelae from Bilet was even preserved in the nearby Kʷiḥa Qirqos church by local clergy, who understood it to be a relic from "ancient Israel" (Smidt 2004).

Lastly, we may note that these communities, whether at Dahlak, Bilet, or Arra, were closely tied to the reinvigorated Red Sea trade that followed the Fatimid Caliphate's push to reassert control over the maritime "silk road." Their gravestones bear witness to the fact that the men and women of Bilet and Dahlak practiced Shīʿism. They also appear to have exhibited sympathies for Ismāʿīlīsm, suggesting a connection to Egypt's new rulers. The new archaeological findings fit well into the larger history of the region known from Egyptian written sources. As we shall see later, the Fatimids became greatly concerned with the Muslim communities of the Ethiopian-Eritrean highlands by the late eleventh century – so much so that they sought to tie the appointment of an Ethiopian metropolitan to the establishment of mosques in the "lands of *al-Ḥabaša*."

The "Affair of the Mosques," or; A Coptic Metropolitan Builds Mosques in "Ethiopia"

Approximately 100 years after the first funerary stelae were laid at Bilet, its Muslim community of both locals and immigrants from places far beyond the Horn of Africa had grown substantially enough to attract the attention of Badr al-Ǧamālī (1073–1094), the Fatimid vizier and *de facto* ruler of Egypt. An evocative episode relating to Ethiopian and Eritrean history has come down to us, again, through the "History of the Patriarchs." It offers a view on how Fatimid economic and religious aspirations, Coptic political maneuverings, and community responses in the Christian highlands eventually resulted in a perfect political storm. Derat, who published a comprehensive investigation into this incident, aptly termed it the "Affair of the Mosques" (Derat 2020b).

What had happened? In the late eleventh century, specifically sometime in 1089/90 CE, vizier Badr al-Ǧamālī heavily involved himself in the appointment of the new "Ethiopian" metropolitan. Somewhat counterintuitively, this maneuver appears to have been part of a larger strategy to bolster the Caliphate's trading endeavors while disseminating Fatimid religious doctrine throughout the Red Sea and the Horn of Africa – an initiative presumably aimed at offsetting recent losses of influence in the largely Sunni-ruled Levant.

The vizier's actions aligned with the Fatimids' agenda of religious proselytization through *da'wa*, religious missions aiming to propagate Ismāʿīlīsm, the branch of Shīʿa Islam championed by the Fatimids. As we saw earlier, at least one Shīʿite trading settlement had been established in the Ethiopian-Eritrean highlands by the late tenth century. A hundred years later, Badr al-Ǧamālī, a former military slave (*mamlūk*) of Armenian Christian descent, sought to ensure that such highland communities maintained their adherence to Shīʿism, and specifically Ismāʿīlīsm – while guaranteeing the steady flow of products passing from Dahlak and the Ethiopian interior to Cairo's markets: Indian and Yemenite textiles, pelts, furs, civet musk, and the enslaved (Derat 2020b, ss. 29–30; Muehlbauer 2021, 10–11).

To achieve this, Badr al-Ǧamālī exploited the influence of the Coptic patriarchate over its dependencies in Nubia and the Horn. He essentially placed Patriarch Cyril II under house arrest, forcing him to relocate from his traditional seat in Alexandria to the Fatimid capital of Cairo, and forbade him from leaving the city without his approval. Cyril II was granted a ceremonial role at the vizier's court, to be summoned at will. Still, he was also given honorary titles and privileges for his community in return for his cooperation (Bramoullé 2020, 168, 533, 555–63).

We need to read the subsequent selection of a rather unusual candidate – a certain Sawīrus – as metropolitan of "Ethiopia" in the 1080s against this broader political backdrop: Sawīrus was not a member of one of the Coptic monastic communities in Egypt; rather, he was the nephew of a previous Ethiopian Christian metropolitan called Victor. To secure the position, Sawīrus appears to have sought the support of the Fatimid vizier rather than that of Patriarch Cyril II. According to the "History," Sawīrus assured Badr al-Ǧamālī that, if he were appointed metropolitan, he would facilitate the construction of mosques in the Ethiopian-Eritrean highlands and protect Muslim merchants in the region. Sawīrus, moreover, committed himself to sending gifts to Cairo from "Ethiopia" and even suggested that he would persuade its Christian king to acknowledge Fatimid sovereignty. By aligning himself with Fatimid interests and leveraging the vizier's support for his appointment, Sawīrus shifted the delicate power dynamics that made the Christian kingdom in the Horn of Africa a bishopric of the Coptic church, subtly tilting the scales in favor of the Fatimids.

Things did not proceed as smoothly as the new metropolitan might have hoped. After his appointment to the Ethiopian see, Sawīrus sent his brother Riğal back to Egypt with gifts for the Fatimid vizier. These offerings, however, were deemed insufficient by Badr al-Ğamālī, who summoned both Patriarch Cyril II and Riğal to demand accountability for the promises tied to Sawīrus's appointment. The list of the vizier's grievances was long: the gifts were inadequate; Sawīrus now owed money to the Fatimids; Muslim traders under Fatimid protection in the Horn of Africa had not been sufficiently protected – in fact, Riğal himself was accused of having plundered a Fatimid-aligned merchant; and, most critically, the promised mosques had not been built (Derat 2020b, s. 8).

Riğal defended his brother by claiming that metropolitan Sawīrus had built seven mosques in the Ethiopian-Eritrean highlands, only to see them rapidly demolished by the understandably confused Christian locals. The latter had shown little understanding as to why their newly appointed ecclesiastical leader was prioritizing the construction of places of worship for a different faith. According to the "History," they had even tried to kill Sawīrus for his actions. When the Christian king of Ethiopia heard of these events, he promptly arrested and imprisoned the metropolitan. As it turned out, Riğal's journey to Cairo in the late 1080s was thus less about delivering gifts and more about seeking the Fatimid vizier's intervention to help secure his brother's freedom (Sāwīris ibn al-Muqaffaʿ 1970, 350).[22]

In response to this chaotic situation, vizier Badr al-Ğamālī instructed Patriarch Cyril II to write a letter to the unnamed Christian king in the Horn of Africa. He demanded the construction of mosques, protection for Muslim traders, and payment of tributary gifts. If the demands were not met, the mother church in Egypt itself would face destruction. Two other Coptic bishops were copied into the exchange, underlining the seriousness of the vizier's threats. Still, the "Ethiopian" king was not easily intimidated. He retorted with a threat of his own – if so much as a single stone was removed from an Egyptian church, he would level Mecca, Islam's holiest site (Derat 2020b, s. 9).

---

[22] In fact, the mosques that Sawīrus was reported to have built, or any building that served the Islamic population of the period, remain enigmatic. Archaeologists have not yet been able to identify a single mosque from this era in the region. Yet, a monumental frieze with large Kufic letters, seemingly dating to the eleventh century, has long been preserved in the church of Wəqro Qirqos, built at the same time about twenty miles north of Bilet (see Figure 3). Its presence and fine workmanship indicate the existence of at least one prestigious mosque in the vicinity, though only one of these seemingly coeval buildings has survived the ravages of time (Muehlbauer 2021; Smidt 2009).

Here, an ecclesiastical appointment within the sprawling territories of the Coptic church – which, despite operating under Muslim rule in Egypt after 640 CE, had several sovereign Christian dependencies under its authority throughout the medieval period – spiraled into something else: the threat of a potentially highly volatile conflict between the Muslim ruler of Egypt and the Christian king of the highlands. At its heart, this conflict seems to have been caused by the personal ambitions of Sawīrus, the Ethiopian-raised Copt from a prestigious Egyptian family who aspired to be metropolitan in the Horn. If anything, the incident now known as the "Affair of the Mosques" also underscores the entangled nature of this religiously diverse part of the medieval world of Afro-Eurasia (Seignobos 2020). It reveals the complex web of coexistence, cooperation, and dependence that tied different and highly heterogeneous communities together in eleventh-century northern Ethiopia, Eritrea, and Egypt (see Figure 3).

Derat suggests that this episode would eventually significantly influence subsequent appointments to the office of metropolitan. From the twelfth century onwards, only Egyptian monks with close connections to the mother church were appointed to the highlands. By choosing metropolitans from within its ranks, the patriarchate managed to reclaim some independence from Egyptian Muslim authorities and "Ethiopian" rulers. Nevertheless, such a shift necessitated regular and consistent interactions. The Mamlūk Egyptian author and historian al-Maqrīzī, writing some 300 years later, notes that Fatimid delegations regularly entered the highlands following Badr al-Ǧamālī's viziership (Derat 2020a, 39; 2020b, s. 18; Muehlbauer 2023b, 137).

Figure 3 Inscribed Kufic block from a Fatimid-era Mosque, eleventh century, preserved in the church of Wəqro Qirqos, Tigray, Ethiopia.

Source: © Photo by Ewa Balicka-Witakowska 2007, DEEDs Project: EWB-2007.002:839.

Revitalized Christian Communities

Despite the scarcity of written sources, preliminary material evidence and the archaeological record suggest a period of political centralization and re-Christianization in northern Ethiopia in the eleventh and twelfth centuries. By that time, the tumultuous rule of the queen of the *Banū l-Ham(u)wīya* was a distant memory. Christian sovereignty had – at least partially – been restored enough that the appointment of a new metropolitan in the region was of interest to the rulers of Egypt and even held the potential to incite a larger conflict. Indeed, the Christian inhabitants of the Ethiopian-Eritrean *ḥaṣani* kingdom (or kingdoms) were reaping benefits from their relations with Fatimid Egypt by the mid eleventh century. These communities, notably adjacent to Muslim trading settlements like that of Bilet, derived considerable wealth from trade connections across the extended Red Sea. Goods, from salt, pelts, civet musk, gold, ivory, and exotic hides to animals (including hippopotami, monkeys, and giraffes) and the enslaved, were exported from the Ethiopian interior to Egypt and beyond (Lepage 2006, 37–38). It is no coincidence that Islamic settlements and, as we shall see, large cruciform basilicas attesting to the new prosperity of local Christian communities were both being built near the same trade routes in the eleventh century.

Fatimid investments in Red Sea routes saw marked improvements in travel conditions, facilitating safe and uninterrupted journeys from the Ethiopian-Eritrean highlands to Egypt. The same seemingly applied to pilgrimages to the Holy Land: highland travelers are attested through their graffiti at renowned monasteries such as the White and Red Monastery in Upper Egypt, the Nile Delta, and the Sinai Peninsula. In the Eastern Mediterranean, traders and pilgrims from the Horn of Africa would have met thriving Christian communities. In Ephesus, Constantinople, and Cyprus, they would have encountered the splendor of the Eastern Roman Empire, including late antique Byzantine cruciform basilicas locally associated with Emperor Justinian.[23]

As noted earlier, local written records allowing a view on Christian society in the Ethiopian-Eritrean highlands for this time remain exceedingly scarce. But there is architectural evidence, and it attests to a time of economic, cultural, and religious revival in the eleventh and twelfth centuries. In a monograph exploring the rock-cut cruciform churches of northern Ethiopia, Mikael Muehlbauer suggests that revitalized Christian elites – following in the footsteps of *ḥaṣani*

---

[23] Muehlbauer suggests that this connection likely invoked powerful associations with Aksumite king Kaleb's conquest of Himyar, undertaken during Justinian's reign, for contemporary highland Christians. The Ethiopian Church had long venerated Kaleb and his son Gäbrä Mäsqäl as saintly figures. Constructing reimagined late antique churches and especially cruciform basilicas adorned with Aksumite architectural features would have allowed these Christian elites to lay claim, or reclaim, the legacy of Aksum at the height of its power (Muehlbauer 2023b, 145).

Danəʾel, who repurposed an old Aksumite throne base to inscribe his victories – embarked on a grand ecclesiastical building campaign in what is now modern-day Tigray. Monumental cruciform churches, carved from the living rock between c. 1050 CE and c. 1150 CE, indicate a flurry of pious activity enabled by trade profits right around the time of the infamous "Affair of the Mosques" (Muehlbauer 2023b).

A notable example is the grand church of Abrəha wä-Aṣbəḥa, at the intersection of the great northern trade route with the open plains of the Gärʿalta mountains (see Figure 4). The church is one of a handful of semi-monolithic aisled and vaulted cruciform basilicas from this period, meticulously cut from a red sandstone escarpment. As evidenced by the many small-scale churches "built" in this manner in southern Eritrea and northern Ethiopia from the eighth century onwards, rock-carving had long been a practical and economical method of constructing churches in the region. While the basilicas of the eleventh and twelfth centuries were similarly located on or just off the old trade corridor that connected the hinterland with the coast, they were conceived on a vastly grander scale: the ceiling of Abrəha wä-Aṣbəḥa rises close to twenty-five feet at its highest point, and its aisles stretch nearly eighty feet from end to end (Muehlbauer 2023b, ch. 2).[24] These dimensions, impressive for any church built in eleventh-century Afro-Eurasia, indicate the substantial resources invested in the church's creation (Lepage and Mercier 2005, 71–91; Muehlbauer 2023b, 19–20, 79–80; Playne 1954, 73–80).

The basilicas of Abrəha wä-Aṣbəḥa, Wəqro Qirqos, and Mikaʾel Amba were all hewn in close proximity to (and within years of) each other. They innovatively blended older Aksumite architectural elements – friezes, blind windows, moldings, lintels – with advanced engineering techniques from contemporary Fatimid Egypt. These techniques notably included barrel vaults and domed cubes, features popularized under the rule of Badr al-Ǧamālī, the Fatimid vizier known for his interest in the Muslim communities of the Ethiopian highlands. Meanwhile, Badr al-Ǧamālī had engaged Armenian architects to fortify Cairo; their designs of city walls and gates mirrored late antique Byzantine fortifications. From there, the novel features transitioned from public spaces to religious ones, adorning Fatimid mosques before being incorporated into the design of

---

[24] Muehlbauer proposes that the commanding design of these eleventh- and twelfth-century structures was far from arbitrary: they were carefully crafted to echo late antique aisled cruciform basilicas, as seen through the lens of contemporary highland elites. This architectural style had been a popular choice for church construction in both the Eastern Mediterranean and the Aksumite kingdom in Late Antiquity. Notably, Aksum's rulers had commissioned such grand edifices not only within the Ethiopian-Eritrean highlands – including Aksum itself – but also in Ṣanʿāʾ in today's Yemen, which came under Aksumite control following the conquest of Himyar in the first half of the sixth century (Muehlbauer 2023b, ch. 1).

Figure 4 Interior view of the Church of Abrəha wä-Aṣbəḥa near Wəqro,
Tigray, Ethiopia.

Source: © Photo by Mikael Muehlbauer 2019.

Coptic churches and centers of worship (Muehlbauer 2023b, 150–54). The
rock-hewn churches of the Tigrayan highlands, constructed primarily in the
last decade of the eleventh century, are thus a testament to the dynamic
exchange of architectural ideas in the extended Eastern Mediterranean. They
echo an Armenian interpretation of Byzantine architectural elements, further
reimagined within contemporary Fatimid Muslim and Coptic structures, modified to include Aksumite features. In the interconnected world of medieval
Afro-Eurasia, artistic production and technological innovation moved fluidly
across religious and cultural boundaries, from Asia Minor to Egypt to the
Ethiopian-Eritrean highlands. The remarkable architecture of Abrəha wä-
Aṣbəḥa bears witness to this early transculturalism.

   Furthermore, the architectural ornamentation of these Christian centers was
seemingly inspired by patterns on Indian, Egyptian, and Armenian fabrics. Such

textiles were traded to the Ethiopian and Eritrean highlands via the same Fatimid trade routes and Muslim networks whose trade surpluses had likely enabled the construction of large-scale churches in the first place. If anything, edifices like Abrəha wä-Aṣbəḥa, Wəqro Qirqos, and Mikaʾel Amba demonstrate the global reach and cosmopolitan nature of the reinvigorated Christian highland community at the turn of the twelfth century (Muehlbauer 2023b, ch. 4).

The Fabric(s) of the World(s)

The far-reaching and regular contacts between the Christian elites and the larger Muslim world are also evident in the local artisanal production of the time. A wall painting of a *Majestas Domini* in the nave of the early-twelfth-century church of Däbrä Sälam Mikaʾel, for instance, depicts Christ sitting cross-legged on an elaborately patterned cushion. According to Claude Lepage, his robes are of an "Islamic" style that represents Christ as a "heavenly Caliph" (Lepage 2006, 32–33). Conversely, we could also suggest that such a representation simply reflects the local realities of a realm where luxurious cloth and fine textiles had long transcended religious and cultural boundaries.

In fact, the presence of imported fabrics from the Islamicate world into medieval Ethiopia and Eritrea has long been documented. During the fascist Italian occupation of the highland plateau (1936–41), colonial ethnographer Antonio Mordini reported discovering a veritable treasure trove of ancient and medieval relics during his visit to the monastery of Däbrä Dammo in August 1939: several storerooms, as well as the monastery's sacristy, harbored thousands of ancient parchment sheets, manuscripts, coins, and a "great quantity" of colorful, precious, richly ornate "Muslim" textiles.

Despite their considerable age, these fabrics were excellently preserved. According to Mordini, most originated from Fatimid Egypt, with several dating back to the pre-Fatimid era. Some had come from the Levant or Yemen. And yet, even though these textiles bore the names of Caliphs and Muslim rulers, inscribed in Arabic, they had been brought to and kept for centuries in Tigray's oldest and most venerated monastery (Mordini 1957).[25] It is possible that some were brought from Egypt by official Coptic delegations, such as the embassy that helped revive the Ethiopian Church following the reign of the queen of the *Banū l-Ham(u)wīya* in the last decades of the tenth century. Others might have come with the mosque-building metropolitan Sawīrus, or vizier Badr al-Ǧamālī's Fatimid embassies

---

[25] Sadly, our ability to now access these materials is largely limited: many of the coins were melted down, and the fabrics were sold on to Egypt as antique collector's items – some as prime examples of ancient Egyptian textile production – by the 1940s (Matthews and Mordini 1959, 50–51; Mordini 1957, 75–76).

following the 1080s CE. Already in the mid twentieth century, however, Mordini speculated that a notable and wealthy Muslim community must have lived near Däbrä Dammo (Matthews and Mordini 1959, 54–55). As we saw earlier, recent archaeological research has partially confirmed his assumption: we now know that heterogeneous and cosmopolitan communities of different faiths thrived between the tenth and the twelfth centuries in Eritrea and northern Ethiopia.

Either way, luxury textiles from faraway lands, whether their patterns were traced in stone, painted onto a seated Christ, or stored in the sacristy of one of Ethiopia's most important monasteries, bear witness to the expansive ties that bound the Ethiopian-Eritrean highlands to the Dahlak archipelago and the Red Sea, and from there to a wider medieval world. If churches like Wəqro Qirqos and the storerooms of Däbrä Dammo reflect the sophisticated tastes and wealth of Christian highland elites, it was the region's Muslim communities – from coastal Dahlak to highland Bilet – that enabled their participation in this long-distance exchange (compare Figures 2 and 3). Within decades, as we shall see, this cultural revival would spark processes of state formation that were unprecedented since Aksumite times.

6 Formation: Conquest, Consolidation, and Commerce, Twelfth–Fifteenth Centuries

The twelfth to fifteenth centuries were marked by a significant expansion of Christian sovereignty in the central highland plateau, which would soon extend far beyond the northern territories that have thus far been our focus. This expansion was not limited to mere geography. Even though there is a conspicuous scarcity of written records, material evidence suggests the formation of a politically sophisticated Christian state stretching from the Eritrean coast deep into the highlands by the mid twelfth century. For once, the dearth of documentation does not seem owed to a lack of contemporary writing; instead, it appears to be the result of a later, systematic destruction of records. The texts that have survived and come down to us present a highly developed administration that governed territories across some 400 miles by the late 1100s CE. Yet, as we shall see, successive territorial expansions by Christian realms in the process of state formation also came at a cost to neighboring communities, particularly if these adhered to a different faith.

The "Great Men of Bəgʷəna": The Zagʷe Dynasty

Traditionally, the Christian polity that stretched over significant portions of the Ethiopian-Eritrean highlands in the twelfth and thirteenth centuries has been associated with the kings of the so-called Zagʷe dynasty. This term, while long established in scholarship, is somewhat misleading: it is an anachronistic exonym of unclear origin that is first documented more than a century after the dynasty was overthrown by Christian rivals. Indeed, it is absent from both local contemporary records and Egyptian sources. New research has revealed that the "Zag^{w}e" kings referred to themselves, their ruling class, and perhaps even the kingdom itself as "[of] Bəg^{w}əna" (Derat 2020a, 45–47).[26] Moreover, recent historical and archaeological scholarship has questioned firmly held academic beliefs about the identity, language, and geographic origin of the Zag^{w}e dynasty, showing that many long-standing assumptions were based on nineteenth- and early-twentieth-century readings of significantly later records (Derat 2018; Derat et al. 2021; Muehlbauer 2023a). This shift becomes evident when we consider recent findings challenging the belief that the Zag^{w}e were Agäw and thus belonged to a Cushitic language group. In fact, all surviving Zag^{w}e sources were composed in Gəʿəz, the ancient and Semitic liturgical language of Aksum and the Ethiopian Church, which ceased to be spoken around the turn of the millennium. Some land grants of the 1100s CE even contained words in Təgrəñña, the language of contemporary Tigray and Eritrea, rather than the far more southerly Agäw. Within the last decade, scholarly consensus holds that there is little to no concrete evidence to support the assertion that the Zag^{w}e were of Agäw origin (Derat 2018, 242–56; 2020a, 50).

To this day, much remains enigmatic about the rulers of the "Zag^{w}e" dynasty. Recently discovered twelfth- and early-thirteenth-century land grants, property registers, and dedicatory inscriptions, however, offer fresh insights into the reigns of two Zag^{w}e kings: Ṭänṭäwədəm and Lalibala (Derat 2010; 2018, 261–72).[27] Despite the fragmentary nature of our sources, it has become evident that the dominion of these Zag^{w}e monarchs (or, more aptly, the territory governed by the "great men of Bəg^{w}əna"[28]) spanned a vast stretch of the highland plateau. Previously, the kingdom was thought to center on the city of Lalibäla in today's North Wollo Zone of the Amhara regional state of Ethiopia, far south of the territories of late antique Aksum and the lands ruled by earlier *ḥaṣani* kings. As we know today, things weren't quite that simple. The surviving sources produced by the Zag^{w}e kings themselves, preserved in both monasteries in the Ethiopian-Eritrean borderlands and the churches of Lalibäla hundreds of

---

[26] From the sixteenth century until today, "Bəg^{w}əna" has simply denoted a district adjacent to Lasta, where the town and churches of Lalibäla are located (Derat 2009). Earlier usage does not reflect this geographic limitation, as northern administrative regions and aristocracy in today's Eritrea were also subsumed under the term at the time of King Lalibala himself (Derat 2020a, 46).

[27] Notably, both kings bore the title *ḥaṣani*, which, however, in contrast to earlier centuries, now indicated the highest power in a realm with a highly sophisticated administrative structure.

[28] Thus identified in the witness-lists to the land donations of both Lalibala and Ṭänṭäwədəm (Derat 2020a, 45–46).

miles to the south, indicate, for instance, that twelfth-century King Ṭänṭäwədəm outlined military activities and the deployment of numerous officers in today's Tigray, a regional state of Ethiopia. King Lalibala, in the early thirteenth century, issued similar documents, one of which names an administrator with the title *baḥər nägaśi*, or "king of the coast," indicating dominion over the littoral of what is now Eritrea. King Lalibala's wife, Queen Mäsqäl Kəbra, was often referred to as the "Lady of Biḥat," a locality in present-day Eritrea near the village of Ham. Her title suggests significant influence over these northernmost areas of the highland plateau, the very region where Christianity had persisted after the decline of the Aksumite kingdom (Derat 2020a).

Despite his wife's northern connections and his ancestor's use of Təgrəñña, King Lalibala is renowned for constructing numerous monumental monolithic churches and buildings in the southerly historical region of Lasta at the turn of the thirteenth century. These structures, meticulously hewn from the native reddish volcanic rock, demonstrate the considerable resources at the Zagᵂe kings' disposal (see Figure 5). Their murals and furnishings display the kingdom's contemporary connections to Coptic Egypt alongside architectural elements from late antique Aksum (Finneran 2009; Mercier and Lepage 2012). The town of Wärwär, subsequently named "Lalibäla" after the king who enabled the churches' construction and designated a UNESCO World Heritage Site in 1978,[29] clearly held great significance for King Lalibala: he dedicated nine altars here. The architectural complexity of Lalibäla, its dozen churches and chapels connected by trenches carved deep into the stone, suggests its deliberate design as a Christian pilgrimage center, possibly modeled after the holy city of Jerusalem. Recent archaeological discoveries furthermore revealed that the town and the churches were built over sites of an earlier, non-Christian, troglodytic culture, suggesting that the territory had only recently come under Zagᵂe control by the 1200s CE (Bosc-Tiessé et al. 2014; Derat et al. 2021). All in all, it seems that Lalibäla and the region of Lasta, long presumed to be the heartland of Zagᵂe power, were, in fact, a frontier zone deliberately transformed into the spiritual heart of the kingdom in the early thirteenth century.

We now know that the dynasty also invested heavily in the realm's religious infrastructure, and refurbished churches in Tigray and Eritrea that dated back to the Aksumite period. By the mid twelfth century, a new metropolitan seat had been established at Maryam Nazret, about thirty miles south of present-day Mekelle. The site, strategically located midway between Lasta and the Red Sea

---

[29] The full name of UNESCO is the United Nations Educational, Scientific and Cultural Organization.

Figure 5 Exterior views of the Zag^we Church of Betä Giyorgis in Lalibäla, Lasta, Ethiopia.

Source: © Photo by Michael Gervers 1993, DEEDs Project: MG-1993.032:008/013.

coast, lay along an extension of the ancient trade route that had witnessed the development of rock-hewn churches and Muslim settlements in previous centuries. The now largely ruined cathedral at Maryam Nazret was once a grand structure – a five-aisled basilica built upon a 100-foot-long Aksumite platform, supported by spolia piers. Coptic metropolitan Mikaʾel, who had been appointed to the highlands by the 1120s CE, initiated the building of the cathedral shortly after his arrival. Its five altar chambers, crowned with domes and a triumphant arch, combined local stylistic and iconographic preferences with architectural elements that were fashionable in twelfth-century Egypt, likely the result of the tastes of Egyptian craftsmen traveling in the metropolitan's entourage (Derat et al. 2020; Muehlbauer 2023a; 2023b, 45–46).

Contemporary records likewise show that the Zag^we kings strove to present themselves as successors to the region's preceding Christian realms in words and deeds. In the mid twelfth century, potentially during King Ṭänṭäwədəm's reign, metropolitan Mikaʾel reconsecrated the vaulted cruciform basilica of Mikaʾel Amba in Eastern Tigray, carved from the living rock by the elites of the *ḥaṣani* kingdom(s) about fifty years earlier. Similarly, the Zagʷe kings refurbished the cathedral in the old capital of Aksum, and their churches, whether in Lalibäla or Nazret, consistently featured Aksumite architectural elements, with some even constructed atop Aksumite monuments.

Such monumental endeavors were paralleled by a deliberate emulation in governance. Recent research shows that the Zagʷe dynasty conscientiously adopted the language of Christian Aksum in its administrative practices and public declarations. Both King Ṭänṭäwədəm and King Lalibala employed a form of Gəʿəz that deliberately echoed phrases from Aksumite epigraphy to administer their kingdom. In his land grants, King Lalibala not only emulated the language of early Aksumite kings but also styled himself as King ʿEzana had done in the fourth century, thereby underscoring both his Christian faith and his claim to Aksum's heritage (Derat 2020a, 52).

These strong claims to continuity were disrupted only by a new Christian dynasty, whose founder overthrew the last Zagʷe king in 1270 CE. Originally named the "lord of the land of Amhara" (*ṣāḥib bilād Amḥara*) or "lord of Amhara" in documents of the Mamlūk chancellery in Egypt (Loiseau 2019b, 639), this dynasty indeed had more southern and rather regional roots, hailing from an area just south of Lalibäla and Lasta. Within a few short decades, its kings – known as the "Solomonic" or "Solomonid" kings in scholarship – would similarly come to portray themselves as the legitimate successors to Aksum. Through their foundational dynastic text, the *Kəbrä nägäśt*, these kings fashioned themselves into the spiritual and genealogical heirs of a supposed son of the biblical king Solomon and the Queen of Sheba. It has been suggested that these new rulers, likely seeking to reinforce their own claims to the throne, erased the records of their predecessors in an intentional act of *damnatio memoriae*. Indeed, as we saw earlier, few records of the once-sophisticated Zagʷe administration have survived. More than 100 years after the end of Zagʷe rule, new sources claiming contemporary authority on the dynasty were composed: by the fifteenth century, the "lives" and histories of the Zagʷe kings were written by scribes working for the Solomonic elite. Thus, the "kings of Bəgʷəna" were renamed and became known as the "Zagʷe," and cast into the role of pious usurpers who had come to power illegitimately. They were also othered for their supposedly strange language and origin – yet simultaneously canonized as saints due to their many holy deeds, such as the construction of the churches in Lalibäla. Here, the history of Ethiopia and Eritrea in the twelfth and thirteenth centuries was, rather literally, rewritten – to an extent that modern historiography is only now beginning to uncover (Derat 2020a, 54–56).

A Christian "Israel": The Solomonic Dynasty

In 1270 CE, a man named Yəkunno Amlak overthrew the last Zagʷe king and established the so-called Solomonic dynasty. His direct descendants would rule over considerable sections of the Ethiopian-Eritrean highland plateau for the following centuries. As late as 1974, Ethiopian Emperor Haile Selassie still claimed lineage from Yəkunno Amlak, underscoring the enduring mythos of the dynasty first established some 700 years earlier.

Yet, the origins of this royal house were far humbler: as noted earlier, Arabic sources from Egypt initially identified the new Christian king of the highlands as the "lord of (the land of) Amhara" (Loiseau 2019b, 639). Amhara, first Christianized by monastic communities from the more northerly reaches of the Horn of Africa at the turn of the millennium, had once been a peripheral polity abutting Zagʷe territory (Derat 2003, 7; Taddesse Tamrat 1972, 35). Our understanding of the changeover of power from the Zagʷe to the Solomonic kings remains limited, but what we may say is that within a few short decades, Yəkunno Amlak's sons and grandsons would dramatically enlarge the Christian territory far beyond their initial core areas, or the kingdom once governed by the Zagʷe dynasty.

The reign of King ʿAmdä Ṣəyon (1314–1344), Yəkunno Amlak's grandson, especially stands out for the dynasty's policy of aggressive expansion. According to a note preserved in a fourteenth-century manuscript of the four gospels at the monastery of Däbrä Ḥayq Ǝsṭifanos itself a Zagʷe foundation, ʿAmdä Ṣəyon launched his wars of conquest in the late 1310s CE. First, the young king annexed parts of the local-religious or "pagan" kingdom of Damot – which had numerous tributaries – and the Muslim Sultanate of Hadiyya in the far south. From there, his troops took the western fringes of the highland plateau in Goǧǧam. Then, they moved north. In what is now Tigray, ʿAmdä Ṣəyon sacked the realms of several Christian rivals – including the city of Aksum – to solidify his claim to the throne (Taddesse Tamrat 1970; 1972). In his own words, ʿAmdä Ṣəyon's dominion now reached as far as the shores of the Red Sea, from where he "mounted an elephant and entered the sea" to sack the Dahlak islands, which had ceased to be an independent sultanate decades earlier (Taddesse Tamrat 1970, 96). In the late 1320s and early 1330s, subsequent campaigns brought most of the central highland plateau firmly under ʿAmdä Ṣəyon's and thus Christian control (Huntingford 1965).

Local Gəʿəz sources, which include land grants, historical notes, religious texts, and even royal chronicles, become comparatively abundant from the late fourteenth century onwards. Many of these texts were composed to portray a very specific perspective: their writers were often closely aligned with the politics and beliefs of the Solomonic house. Yet, from the early 1400s onwards, Christian Gəʿəz and Latin as well as Arabic sources from the Islamicate world agree that the Solomonic kings ruled supreme over numerous regional powers and several non-Christian, mainly Muslim, tributaries (Chekroun and Hirsch 2020b; Deresse Ayenachew 2020). Nearly a thousand miles long and several hundred miles wide, their claimed territory stretched from the Red Sea to areas south of Lake Zʷay, beyond the present-day Ethiopian capital of Addis Ababa, and from the western fringes of the highlands beyond Lake Ṭana to Ifat in the east (Crummey 2000; Deresse Ayenachew 2020). To ensure their dominion, Solomonic rulers strategically stationed *čäwa* military regiments throughout the conquered lands (compare Figure 6). Great numbers of such garrisons were found on the southern and eastern fringes of the central highlands, where Muslim populations of recently annexed Islamic sultanates were now living under Christian suzerainty (Deresse Ayenachew 2014).

Moreover, a number of ideological strategies underpinned the Solomonic expansion in the fourteenth century. A first key element was the rulers' claim of genealogical and spiritual descent from the biblical kings David and Solomon, carefully elaborated in their dynastic myth, the *Kəbrä nägäśt*. Originally a foreign work of Arabic and possibly Coptic provenance, the text had been translated into Gəʿəz by the 1320s CE (Budge 2000; Marrassini 2007). By the late fifteenth century, the worldview and ideology of the *Kəbrä nägäśt* formed the very basis of Solomonic Christian kingship in the highlands. It was widely propagated through texts, images, and even building projects (Gnisci 2020; Krebs 2021, ch. 5). At its core, this myth expands the biblical story of King Solomon and the Queen of Sheba to include the birth of a son, Mənilək, who governed a mighty realm called *Ityoṗya* (ኢትዮጵያ). Recognized by Solomon as his true heir, Mənilək is portrayed as bringing the Ark of the Covenant from the First Temple in Jerusalem to his kingdom of *Ityoṗya*, thereby establishing "Ethiopia" as the new chosen land of God (Budge 2000). This claim to biblical successorship became the cornerstone of Solomonic royal ideology. Drawing, again, from the *Kəbrä nägäśt*, Solomonic kings furthermore asserted that they had reestablished the old Aksumite line. They then cast their predecessors, the Zagʷe, into the role of usurpers, rewriting local history. We may note that references to the local Christian kingdom consistently and explicitly identified the realm, its rulers, and its peoples as that of *Ityoṗya* – "Ethiopia" – from the mid fourteenth century onwards.

Yet, strategies of political legitimization needed to extend beyond the immediate royal house; it was necessary to include the local elites to successfully govern a vast realm. According to Deresse Ayenachew, the rulers promoted a royal ideology called "Shebanization" (አዜብዋነት), which emphasized the

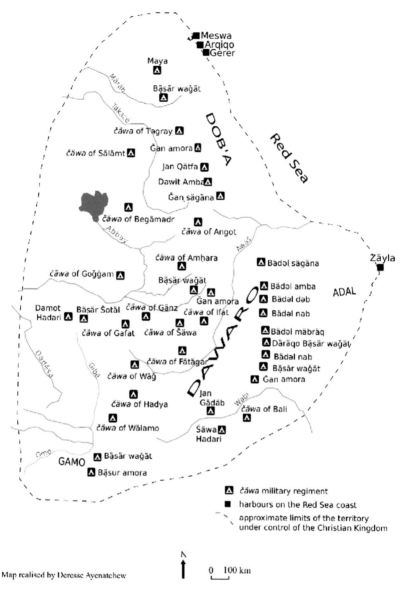

Figure 6 Location of *čäwa* military regiments in the fifteenth century.
Source: © Map by Deresse Ayenachew 2023.

purportedly Judaic roots of pre-Christian highland culture. Local administrators and nobles were said to have been descended from the many councilors that Mənilək had brought with him from Jerusalem in ancient times to successfully govern *Ityoṗya* – said to have settled all over the highlands millennia earlier. Court ceremonials such as the *Śərʿatä mängəśt* accordingly put forth a view on local "history" that allowed for people from diverse regional, linguistic, and religious backgrounds to become ideologically assimilated into the worldview propagated by the Solomonic line (Deresse Ayenachew 2021).

In practical terms, politics and religion were closely intertwined from the dynasty's earliest days. From the late thirteenth century, Solomonic rulers allied with existing monasteries such as Däbrä Ḥayq Ǝsṭifanos and Däbrä ʿAsbo (later renamed Däbrä Libanos). These alliances were fortified through a land tenure system that allowed the kings to endow lands to monastic communities in exchange for service and support. This necessitated positive relations between the monastic communities and the rulers, cultivating a reciprocal relationship where religious leaders significantly influenced Solomonic politics. For instance, the abbot of Däbrä Ḥayq Ǝsṭifanos traditionally held the third-highest court office and served as an advisor to the ruler, while the abbot of Däbrä Libanos held the position of *əččäge*, the highest autochthonous ecclesi-astical office after that of the Egyptian metropolitan (Derat 2003, chs. 3–5). Despite occasional tensions between the royal house and certain monastic movements, all evangelizing efforts by local monks were in the interest of the ruling dynasty (Adankpo-Labadie 2023; Kaplan 1984). Moreover, monasteries served as centers of learning, administration, law, and artistic and ecclesiastical production, providing valuable infrastructure in a realm ruled by a mobile court of 30,000 to 40,000 people that regularly moved through the highlands (Deresse Ayenachew 2009).[30]

In the fifteenth and early sixteenth centuries, Solomonic kings also established numerous royal churches and monasteries, all of which remained under their direct sovereignty (see Figure 7). These prestigious religious centers served as symbols of their divinely ordained power, particularly in regions where Christianity (and, often, Solomonic rule) was a relatively recent introduction. In keeping with the worldview put forth in the *Kəbrä nägäśt*, many of these buildings are thought to have been designed and laid out in a manner mirroring the biblical descriptions of King Solomon's First Temple in Jerusalem (2 Chronicles, 3 and 1 Kings, 6). Although comprehensive surveys and excava-tions of these sites are still pending, the available evidence suggests that most were constructed from finely dressed stone with wooden interiors that were richly adorned with gold paneling, gemstones, and paintings (Krebs 2021, ch. 5).

As a side-effect of all this prodigious royal building, more than a dozen embassies were sent to various Latin Christian courts in Europe between c. 1400 and the late 1520s. Ethiopian ambassadors are attested in Venice, Valencia,

---

[30] The size of the court is given as both 20,000 and 40,000 people in an early sixteenth-century Portuguese source (Beckingham and Huntingford 1961, 268); Gəʿəz sources on the royal banquet indicate the presence of c. 34,500 men and women (Kropp 1988).

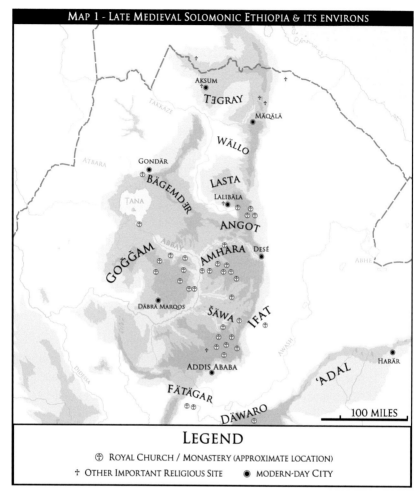

Figure 7 Royal churches and monasteries in Solomonic
Ethiopia, c. 1400–1530

Source: © Map by Verena Krebs 2020.

Naples, Lisbon, and repeatedly in Rome. Meanwhile, Ethiopian pilgrims, sometimes acting in an ambassadorial capacity, traveled to places as varied as Constance in modern-day Germany and Santiago de Compostela in western Iberia. In Europe, Solomonic envoys sought to secure relics, rare liturgical fabrics, and foreign furnishings for the kings' building projects. These embassies again appear to have been a (ritual) emulation of King Solomon's diplomatic practices preceding the building of the First Temple in Jerusalem (2 Chronicles, 2 and 1 Kings, 5). Contrary to long-held scholarly belief, recent research has shown that an interest in European arms, "technology," or military alliances played no role in these early exchanges (Krebs 2021). Moreover, it must be noted that the Solomonic kings held full control over these encounters with the Latin West well into the sixteenth century. They also simultaneously maintained largely amicable and regular diplomatic relations with Muslim powers, such as the Mamlūk Sultanate in Egypt (Krebs 2019; Loiseau 2019b; 2020a).

A lasting shift in these dynamics and interests occurred only in the 1520s CE, following the arrival of the Portuguese and the Ottomans in the Red Sea region and particularly after a series of devastating wars with the neighboring Sultanate of ʿAdal, a former tributary, in the second quarter of the sixteenth century (Chekroun 2016; Stenhouse and Pankhurst 2005). These events permanently shifted the Christian kingdom's internal power structure, economic base, and geographic reach, leading to substantial territorial losses by the early 1600s CE. Only in the late nineteenth century would another Amhara king, Mənilək II of Šäwa, once more attempt to establish rule over a territory as large as that claimed by the Solomonic rulers of the late Middle Ages.

The Disappearance of Muslim Communities in Tigray

Authorities in what is now Eastern Tigray had encouraged and safeguarded Islamic communities during the Christian resurgence leading up to the advent of Zagʷe rule in the early 1100s CE, seeing that they benefited from their extensive trade connections (Loiseau et al. 2021, 524). In the mid twelfth century, when the state-building efforts of the Zagʷe dynasty led to aggressive Christianization campaigns intended to reinforce their right to rule, this relationship began to change. Control over the trade route connecting the Zagʷe territories in Lasta to the Red Sea littoral increasingly fell into Christian hands, and the Muslims whose activities had once fueled the revitalization of the *ḥaṣani* kingdoms found themselves forcibly relocated or expelled from their lands.

A twelfth-century land grant by King Ṭänṭäwədəm exemplifies this shift: here, the Zagʷe king allocated the lands, livestock, and inhabitants of a formerly Muslim area called Ṣəraʿ to the church of Betä Mäsqäl in Qəfrəya. This region, located in Eastern Tigray, encompassed the site of the recently excavated, once-prosperous Islamic settlement of Bilet. King Ṭänṭäwədəm's account indicates a conflict between the Muslims of Ṣəraʿ and the Christian administration, but also suggests that the highland Shīʿite community was progressively losing its wealth and external protection from Egypt. There, Shīʿa communities were facing their own political turmoil: in 1171 CE, Saladin ended the Shīʿite Fatimid Caliphate, and its lands came under Ayyūbīd Sunni rule. Zooming out even further, geopolitical shifts in the wake of the Mongol conquests in Asia would soon direct trade from Red Sea "silk road" routes toward the Persian Gulf. The archaeological data record a decline in Muslim settlements in Tigray in the second half of the twelfth century. By the late 1200s, Bilet and other Islamic sites were fully deserted (Derat 2020b; Loiseau 2020b; Muehlbauer 2023b, 53, 137–38).

Trade and Southern "Frontier" Zones

The history of the more southeasterly Muslim communities of the Ethiopian-Eritrean highland plateau in this period is quite a different story. Two principal trade routes played a vital role in the Islamization of the region. One, as we have seen, originated from the Dahlak Islands and the Eritrean coast, leading east through the highlands of Tigray to the Christian kingdoms in Lasta, Amhara, Šäwa, and onwards to resource-rich local-religious or "pagan" territories such as Damot at its southernmost extent (Bouanga 2014). However, once Christian traders began to dominate this commercial thoroughfare in Zag^{w}e and Solomonic times, a second route gained importance by the late thirteenth century. This trade-way originated in the southwest, linking regions like Damot with the Muslim principalities of Däwaro and Hadiyya before crossing the lowlands of the Sultanate of Ifat and its successor, ʿAdal. Climbing across the Čärčär massif, close to the modern-day cities of Dire Dawa and Harar, this alternate route terminated at the port of Zaylaʿ in modern-day Somaliland (Chekroun et al. 2011).

Written and archaeological sources attest to the exchange of goods along this second route. They included glazed ceramics from China and Southeast Asia, and blown glass, beads, and textiles from Egypt, Central Asia, and South Asia, brought from the coast to the mountains. Commodities such as gold, worked jewelry, shells, glass, textiles, ivory, precious hides, incense, and enslaved individuals were traded in the opposite direction, forming the foundation for the growth and prosperity of several Muslim principalities and local-religious kingdoms. Between the thirteenth and the fifteenth centuries, most of these political entities thrived in the vicinity of, and sometimes as tributaries of, their Christian neighbors (Chekroun and Hirsch 2020b; Insoll 2023).

The Sultanates of Šawah, Ifat, Hadiyya, and ʿAdal

Concurrent with the formation of the "Zag^{w}e" kingdom, a sovereign Muslim polity emerged in the historical record in the twelfth and thirteenth centuries: the Sultanate of Šawah, ruled by the Maḫzūmī family. It was situated on the southern stretch of the trade corridor from Lasta to the Eritrean coast. The area around Šawah appears to have adopted Islam by the eleventh century, possibly influenced by Muslim traders from settlements such as Bilet. While our understanding of this principality remains limited, we know that the inhabitants of Šawah were literate, authoring their own histories in Arabic, and that the community was prosperous enough to support a sophisticated judicial hierarchy (Chekroun and Hirsch 2020b, 93–95; Gori 2020).

By 1285 CE, however, Šawah was destroyed; its ruling family was killed, and its territory and people were annexed by a neighboring Muslim realm, the Sultanate of Ifat. To facilitate its takeover of Šawah, the Walasmaʿ dynasty of Ifat appears to have formed an alliance with the Solomonic kings, who had themselves recently overthrown their Christian rivals, the Zagᵂe. In exchange for this support, Ifat reportedly entered into a tributary agreement with its Christian neighbors (Cerulli 1941). We must note the geographic proximity of these territories, ruled by dynasties of different faiths: the Solomonic heartlands of Šäwa and Amhara were located just a few miles west of Ifat, which occupied the easternmost fringes of the central highland plateau. From this strategic location, facing the Rift Valley and the Afar salt plains, the Walasmaʿ established a secondary trade route that connected the interior of the highlands with the coast.

Over the course of the fourteenth century, the Sultanate of Ifat emerged as the dominant Islamic power in the central highlands. Preliminary archaeological surveys and excavations have uncovered several ruined cities dating from this period, all built in a remarkably uniform manner (Fauvelle, Hirsch, and Chekroun 2017, 278). These centers, protected by city walls, reveal a densely populated and well-organized urban landscape, complete with paved streets and terraced houses. Inside the city limits, numerous neighborhood mosques, alongside grander Friday mosques built from fired brick, testify to a vibrant Islamic culture. The capital, Awfāt, contained an impressive necropolis that included the final resting place of the ruling Walasmaʿ family (Fauvelle, Hirsch, and Chekroun 2017, 288–95). This necropolis was marked by gravestones adorned with monumental Kufic script, commemorating both men and women. Many of these gravestones bore the "Seal of Solomon" as a talismanic ornament, a feature also observed on the funerary stelae from Bilet (Fauvelle-Aymar et al. 2006; Loiseau 2020b).

Much of Ifat's prosperity may be attributed to the growth of the port city of Zaylaʿ in present-day Somaliland. Once a modest coastal trading post, Zaylaʿ had transformed into the terminal point for long-distance trade goods from the highland interior by the turn of the fourteenth century. This development was likely spurred by the political upheaval caused by the Solomonic overthrow of Zagᵂe rule and Ifat's conquest of the Sultanate of Šawah. As Ibn ʿAbd al-Ẓāhir, a Mamlūk chancery scribe in Egypt, noted in the late thirteenth century, the turmoil in the highlands had led to an increased supply of enslaved individuals from "Ethiopia," contributing to Zayla''s rise as a primary hub for their export, particularly to the Eastern Mediterranean, Egypt, the Arabian Peninsula, and the Indian Ocean world (Fauvelle and Hirsch 2011; Fauvelle et al. 2011). Given their involvement in the transport of captives from the highland regions to the Red Sea networks, it is plausible to suggest that the early-fourteenth-century wars of conquest waged by Solomonic king ʿAmdä Ṣəyon enriched both Ifat and Zaylaʿ.[31]

The political status of the Sultanate of Ifat, like that of the smaller Sultanate of Hadiyya, remains somewhat enigmatic. Hadiyya was known for its "production" of enslaved eunuchs, which were highly valued across Afro-Eurasia from Egypt to China, and traded this precious "commodity" predominantly through Ifat. After the takeover of Šawah, Ifat had formally become a tributary of the Christian kingdom (Chekroun and Hirsch 2020b; Wion 2020). Yet, source accounts are contradictory: several Gəʿəz texts from the period indicate that the *amino*, or chief, of the Sultanate of Hadiyya had formed an alliance with the Sultan of Ifat in the 1330s CE to resist the increasingly expansionist policies of Solomonic king ʿAmdä Ṣəyon (Deresse Ayenachew 2011). By the late fourteenth century, Ifat's semi-sovereignty had eroded. In 1403 CE, its last ruler, Sultan Saʿd al-Dīn, was killed by Solomonic king Dawit II, who effectively annexed Ifat for the Christian kingdom. In the aftermath, some members of Saʿd al-Dīn's family fled to Yemen, while others conceded to their lands' integration into the Solomonic realm – certain Walasmaʿ nobles even served in its administration.

In the early 1400s, the mosques of Awfāt were turned into churches by Christian settlers (Fauvelle, Hirsch, and Chekroun 2017, 270). Yet, many of the region's inhabitants remained Muslim, and the Solomonic kings established several military regiments and monasteries as signs of their dominion over the area. As a nominally Christian region, Ifat flourished due to its robust trade, generating substantial wealth for the Solomonic kingdom. Early-sixteenth-century Italian, Portuguese, and Gəʿəz sources attest to its commercial vibrancy, stating that gold coins from Venice and Hungary were common in its bustling markets (Chekroun and Hirsch 2020b, 109).

In the 1420s, the descendants of Saʿd al-Dīn who had fled to Yemen following the sultan's death returned from their exile. On the eastern fringes of what had become the Christian province of Ifat, stretching across the Rift Valley and on to

---

[31] Over the course of the fourteenth and fifteenth centuries, the city of Zaylaʿ would also become an important stopover place for Muslim pilgrims on the *ḥaǧǧ*. Several freeborn "Ethiopian" (*ḥabaša*) student communities at the famous al-Azhar mosque in fifteenth-century Cairo were identified as Zayāliʿa – "coming from Zaylaʿ" (Loiseau 2019a).

the Čärčär mountain plateau, they established a new Muslim principality. Named *Barr Saʿd al-Dīn*, or "land of Saʿd al-Dīn," in honor of their father, the sultanate was ruled by Saʿd al-Dīn's son, Ṣabr al-Dīn. Commonly referred to as the "Sultanate of ʿAdal" in scholarship, this principality resisted subsequent Solomonic efforts to forcefully integrate it into the Christian kingdom. Despite repeated raids and intermittently successful annexation attempts by Solomonic forces throughout the fifteenth century, ʿAdal largely maintained its sovereignty as an Islamic polity. Furthermore, it extended its influence by bringing smaller entities previously affiliated with Muslim Ifat – such as Harlaa and Zaylaʿ – under its control.[32]

By the mid fifteenth century, ʿAdal remained the sole sovereign Muslim power in the Ethiopian-Eritrean highlands. Despite its conflicts with the Solomonic kingdom, the sultanate and its tributaries also traded with the Christian realm. Yet, annual raids between the two powers became routine in the late fifteenth and early sixteenth centuries. In the early 1500s CE, these skirmishes were increasingly fueled by eschatological expectations and the supply of new weapons in the rapidly changing political environment of the Red Sea and Indian Ocean region. In the late 1520s, economically motivated raids escalated into a full-blown war. By 1531, ʿAdali forces had overrun much of the Solomonic Christian kingdom and turned it into a tributary of Muslim sovereignty. Solomonic armies, with the help of Portuguese troops, only managed to reclaim the territory more than a decade later (Chekroun 2016; Chekroun and Hirsch 2020a; Stenhouse and Pankhurst 2005).

By the latter half of the sixteenth century, exhausted from years of warfare, both ʿAdal and the Solomonic Christian kingdom were severely weakened. ʿAdal dwindled to the status of a city-state. The Ottomans eventually incorporated large sections of the Eritrean and the Somaliland coast into their empire (Smidt and Gori 2010). Similarly, with much of its administrative and physical infrastructure in tatters, the Solomonic kingdom found itself the object of Portuguese expansionist desires and Catholic proselytization efforts, ringing in a new phase of Ethiopian-Latin Christian encounters (Cohen 2009; Martinez d'Alos-Moner 2015).

Already in 1520, the soldiers from Portugal had plundered the islands of Dahlak, which centuries earlier had been essential to the growth of both Christian and Muslim communities in the Ethiopian-Eritrean highlands.

---

[32] Harlaa, connected with the historical locality of Hobat, has recently been the site of extensive excavations. This Muslim locality is noteworthy for its extensive long-distance connections between the eleventh and the fifteenth centuries: the archaeological record attests close and manifold ties from the Eastern Mediterranean and Yemen to the Indian Ocean world, and even China (Insoll 2021, 2023; Insoll et al. 2021; Parsons-Morgan 2023; Pryor, Insoll, and Evis 2020).

Shortly after that, Solomonic king Ləbnä Dəngəl permitted the Portuguese crown to build a church and a fort on the islands. There were no more traders on the archipelago that had once helped build the wealth of coastal and highland communities alike. Only soldiers remained (Beckingham and Huntingford 1961, 51, 478–79).

References

Adankpo-Labadie, Olivia. 2023. *Moines, Saints et Hérétiques dans l'Éthiopie Médiévale: Les Disciples d'Ēwosṭātēwos et l'invention d'un Mouvement Monastique Hétérodoxe (XIVe–Milieu du XVe Siècle)*. Rome: École française de Rome.

Alebachew Belay Birru. 2020a. "Megaliths, Landscapes, and Society in the Central Highlands of Ethiopia: An Archaeological Research." PhD thesis, Université Toulouse Jean Jaurès.

——— 2020b. "The 'Shay Culture' Revisited: Overview of Recent Archaeological Fiedlworks in the Central Highlands of Ethiopia." *Nyame Akuma* 39: 11–16.

Andersen, Knud Tage. 2000. "The Queen of the Habasha in Ethiopian History, Tradition and Chronology." *Bulletin of the School of Oriental and African Studies* 63.1: 31–63.

Anfray, Francis. 1974. "Deux Villes Axoumites: Adoulis et Matara." In *IV Congresso Internazionale di Studi Etiopici. Roma 10–15 Aprile 1972*, 745–65. Rome: Accademia nazionale dei Lincei.

Athanasius. 1987. *Athanase d'Alexandrie: Deux Apologies*. Edited by Jan M. Szymusiak. Paris: Éditions du Cerf.

Barnes, T. D. 1976. "The Victories of Constantine." *Zeitschrift Für Papyrologie Und Epigraphik* 20: 149–55.

Bausi, Alessandro. 2021. "'Paleografia quale Scienza dello Spirito': Once More on the Gəʿəz Inscription of Ham (RIÉ No. 232)." In *Exploring Written Artefacts: Objects, Methods, and Concepts*, edited by Jörg B. Quenzer, 3–33. Berlin: De Gruyter.

——— 2023. "'Lingua Franca Notarile Bizantina' in Etiopia? Su un Tratto Linguistico nel Più Antico Testo Documentario Etiopico (Le Costruzioni del Tipo ʾəmfalaga Falagu, 'lungo il Fiume')." In *Documenti Scartati, Documenti Reimpiegati. Forme, Linguaggi, Metodi per Nuove Prospettive di Ricerca*, edited by Giuseppe De Gregorio, Maddalena Modesti, and Marta Luigina Mangini, 309–35. Geneva: Società Ligure di Storia Patria.

Beckingham, Charles F., and George W. B. Huntingford, eds. 1961. *The Prester John of the Indies: A True Relation of the Lands of the Prester John, Being the Narrative of the Portuguese Embassy to Ethiopia in 1520, Written by Father Francisco Alvares*. 2 vols. Cambridge: Cambridge University Press.

Bortolotto, Susanna, Nelly Cattaneo, and Serena Massa. 2021. "Seasonal Watercourses as the Source of Wealth and a Cause of Destruction: The

Water Management in Adulis (Eritrea) in Antiquity and Today." *Larhyss Journal* 47: 25–38.

Bosc-Tiessé, Claire, Marie-Laure Derat, Laurent Bruxelles, François-Xavier Fauvelle, Yves Gleize, and Romain Mensan. 2014. "The Lalibela Rock Hewn Site and Its Landscape (Ethiopia)." *Journal of African Archaeology* 12.2: 141–64.

Bouanga, Ayda. 2014. "Le Royaume du Damot: Enquête sur une Puissance Politique et Économique de la Corne de l'Afrique (XIIIe Siècle)." *Annales d'Éthiopie* 29: 27–58.

Bowersock, G. W. 1971. "A Report on Arabia Provincia." *Journal of Roman Studies* 61: 219–42.

2013. *The Throne of Adulis: Red Sea Wars on the Eve of Islam.* Oxford: Oxford University Press.

Bramoullé, David. 2020. *Les Fatimides et la Mer (909–1171).* Leiden: Brill.

Breton, Jean-François, and Yohannes Aytenew Ayele. 2019. "Kwiha (Tigray, Ethiopia): The Aksumite City." *Afrique: Archéologie & Arts* 15: 53–66.

Budge, E. A. Wallis. 1928. *The Book of the Saints of the Ethiopian Church: A Translation of the Ethiopic Synaxarium Made from the Manuscripts Oriental 660 and 661 in the British Museum.* Cambridge: Cambridge University Press.

2000. *The Queen of Sheba and Her Only Son Menyelek (Kebrä Nägäst).* Repr. Oxford: Oxford University Press.

Burstein, S. M. 1981. "Axum and the Fall of Meroe." *Journal of the American Research Center in Egypt* 18: 47–50.

Casson, Lionel. 1989. *The Periplus Maris Erythraei: Text with Introduction, Translation, and Commentary.* Princeton, NJ: Princeton University Press.

Cerulli, Enrico. 1941. "Il Sultanato dello Scioa nel Secolo XIII Secondo un Nuovo Documento Storico." *Rassegna Di Studi Etiopici* 1.1: 5–42.

Chaniotis, Angelos. 2010. "Megatheism: The Search for the Almighty God and the Competition of Cults." In *One God: Pagan Monotheism in the Roman Empire*, edited by Peter Van Nuffelen and Stephen Mitchell, 112–40. Cambridge: Cambridge University Press.

Chekroun, Amélie. 2016. "Ottomans, Yemenis and the 'Conquest of Abyssinia' (1531–1543)." In *Movements in Ethiopia/Ethiopia in Movement: Proceedings of the 18th International Conference of Ethiopian Studies*, edited by Éloi Ficquet, Ahmed Hassen Omer, and Thomas Osmond, 163–74. Los Angeles, CA: Tsehai.

Chekroun, Amélie, Régis Bernard, Deresse Ayenachew, Hailu Zeleke, Olivier Onezime, Addisu Shewangizaw, François-Xavier Fauvelle, and Bertrand Hirsch. 2011. "Les Harla: Archéologie et Mémoire des

Géants d'Ethiopie: Proposition de Séquence Historique pour les Sites du Čärčär." In *Espaces Musulmans de la Corne de l'Afrique au Moyen Âge*, edited by François-Xavier Fauvelle and Bertrand Hirsch, 75–98. Paris: De Boccard.

Chekroun, Amélie, and Bertrand Hirsch. 2020a. "The Muslim–Christian Wars and the Oromo Expansion: Transformations at the End of the Middle Ages (ca. 1500–ca. 1560)." In *A Companion to Medieval Ethiopia and Eritrea*, edited by Samantha Kelly, 454–76. Leiden: Brill.

2020b. "The Sultanates of Medieval Ethiopia." In *A Companion to Medieval Ethiopia and Eritrea*, edited by Samantha Kelly, 86–112. Leiden: Brill.

Chowdhury, K. A., and G. M. Buth. 1971. "Cotton Seeds from the Neolithic in Egyptian Nubia and the Origin of Old World Cotton." *Biological Journal of the Linnean Society* 3.4: 303–12.

Cohen, Leonardo. 2009. *The Missionary Strategies of the Jesuits in Ethiopia (1555–1632)*. Wiesbaden: Harassowitz.

Conti Rossini, Carlo. 1937. "Necropoli Musulmana ed Antica Chiesa Cristiana Presso Uogrì Haribà nell'Enderta." *Rivista degli Studi Orientali* 17: 399–408.

Crawford, Osbert G. S. 1958. *Ethiopian Itineraries circa 1400–1524: Including Those Collected by Alessandro Zorzi at Venice in the Years 1519–24*. Cambridge: Hakluyt Society.

Crummey, Donald. 2000. *Land and Society in the Christian Kingdom of Ethiopia: From the Thirteenth to the Twentieth Century*. Urbana: University of Illinois Press.

Cuvigny, H., and Christian Julien Robin. 1996. "Des Kinaidokolpite Clans un Ostracon Grec du Desert Oriental (Egypte)." *Topoi* 6.2: 6970720.

Dege-Müller, Sophia. 2018. "Between Heretics and Jews: Inventing Jewish Identities in Ethiopia." *Entangled Religions* 6: 247–308.

Derat, Marie-Laure. 2003. *Le Domaine des Rois Éthiopiens, 1270–1527: Espace, Pouvoir et Monarchisme – Histoire Ancienne et Médiévale*. Paris: Publications de la Sorbonne.

2009. "Du Beg^{w}enā au Lāstā : Centre et Périphérie dans le Royaume d'Éthiopie du XIIIe au XVIe Siècle." *Annales d'Éthiopie* 24: 65–86.

2010. "Les Donations du Roi Lālibalā: Éléments pour une Géographie du Royaume Chrétien d'Éthiopie au Tournant du XIIe et du XIIIe Siècle." *Annales d'Éthiopie* 25: 19–42.

2018. *L'énigme d'une Dynastie Sainte et Usurpatrice Ddans le Royaume Chrétien d'Éthiopie du XIe au XIIIe Siècle*. Hagiologia 14. Turnhout: Brepols.

2020a. "Before the Solomonids: Crisis, Renaissance and the Emergence of the Zagwe Dynasty (Seventh–Thirteenth Centuries)." In *A Companion to*

Medieval Ethiopia and Eritrea, edited by Samantha Kelly, 31–56. Leiden: Brill.

    2020b. "L'affaire des Mosquées." *Médiévales* 79: 15–36.

Derat, Marie-Laure, Claire Bosc-Tiessé, Antoine Garric, Romain Mensan, François-Xavier Fauvelle, Yves Gleize, and Anne-Lise Goujon. 2021. "The Rock-Cut Churches of Lalibela and the Cave Church of Washa Mika'el: Troglodytism and the Christianisation of the Ethiopian Highlands." *Antiquity* 95.380: 467–86.

Derat, Marie-Laure, Emmanuel Fritsch, Claire Bosc-Tiessé, Antoine Garric, Romain Mensan, François-Xavier Fauvelle, and Hiluf Berhe. 2020. "Māryām Nāzrēt (Ethiopia): The Twelfth-Century Transformations of an Aksumite Site in Connection with an Egyptian Christian Community." *Cahiers d'Études Africaines* 239: 473–507.

Deresse Ayenachew. 2009. "Le Kätäma: La Cour et le Camp en Ethiopie (XIVe–XVIe Siècle) – Espace et Pouvoir." PhD thesis, Université de Paris 1 Panthéon-Sorbonne.

    2011. "The Southern Interests of the Royal Court of Ethiopia in the Light of Bərbər Maryam's Ge'ez and Amharic Manuscripts." Special issue with the theme Production, Preservation, and Use of Ethiopian Archives (Fourteenth–Eighteenth Centuries), edited by Anaïs Wion and Paul Bertrand. *Northeast African Studies* 11/2: 43–57.

    2014. "Evolution and Organisation of the Čäwa Military Regiments in Medieval Ethiopia." *Annales d'Éthiopie* 29: 83–95.

    2020. "Territorial Expansion and Administrative Evolution under the 'Solomonic' Dynasty." In *A Companion to Medieval Ethiopia and Eritrea*, edited by Samantha Kelly, 57–85. Leiden: Brill.

    2021. "The Ideology of the Shebanization and the Birth of the Ethiopian Nation (13th–16th Century)." *International Journal of Ethiopian Studies* 14.1/2: 79–104.

el-Chennafi, Mohammed. 1976. "Mention Nouvelle d'une 'Reine Éthiopienne' au IVe s. de l'hégire / Xe s. Ap. J.-C." *Annales d'Éthiopie* 10: 119–21.

Fattovich, Rodolfo. 2014. "La Civiltà Aksumita: Aspetti Archeologici." In *Storia e Leggenda dell'Etiopia Tardoantica: Le Iscrizioni Reali Aksumite*, 273–92. Brescia: Paideia.

Fauvelle, François-Xavier. 2018. *The Golden Rhinoceros: Histories of the African Middle Ages*. Princeton, NJ: Princeton University Press.

    2020. "Of Conversion and Conversation: Followers of Local Religions in Medieval Ethiopia." In *A Companion to Medieval Ethiopia and Eritrea*, edited by Samantha Kelly, 113–41. Leiden: Brill.

Fauvelle, François-Xavier, and Bertrand Hirsch. 2011. "En Guise d'introduction: Sur les Traces de l'Islam Ancien en Éthiopie et dans la Corne de l'Afrique." In *Espaces Musulmans de la Corne de l'Afrique au Moyen Âge*, edited by François-Xavier Fauvelle and Bertrand Hirsch, 11–26. Paris: De Boccard.

Fauvelle, François-Xavier, Bertrand Hirsch, Régis Bernard, and Frédéric Champagne. 2011. "Le Port de Zeyla et Son Arrière-Pays au Moyen Âge: Investigations Archéologiques et Retour aux Sources Écrites." In *Espaces Musulmans de la Corne de l'Afrique au Moyen Âge*, edited by François-Xavier Fauvelle and Bertrand Hirsch, 27–74. Paris: De Boccard.

Fauvelle, François-Xavier, Bertrand Hirsch, and Amélie Chekroun. 2017. "Le Sultanat de l'Awfāt, Sa Capitale et La Nécropole Des Walasma'." *Annales Islamologiques* 51: 239–95.

Fauvelle, François-Xavier, and Bertrand Poissonnier. 2012. *La Culture Shay d'Éthiopie: Recherches Archéologiques et Historiques sur une Élite Païenne*. Paris: De Boccard.

Fauvelle-Aymar, François-Xavier, and Bertrand Hirsch. 2004. "Muslim Historical Spaces in Ethiopia and the Horn of Africa: A Reassessment." *Northeast African Studies* 11.1: 25–53.

Fauvelle-Aymar, François-Xavier, Bertrand Hirsch, Laurent Bruxelles, Chalachew Mesfin, and Amélie Chekroun. 2006. "Reconnaissance de Trois Villes Musulmanes de l'époque Médiévale dans l'Ifat." *Annales d'Éthiopie* 22: 133–75.

Finneran, Niall. 2009. "Built by Angels? Towards a Buildings Archaeology Context for the Rock-Hewn Medieval Churches of Ethiopia." *World Archaeology* 41.3: 415–29.

Gaventa, Beverly Roberts. 1986. *From Darkness to Light: Aspects of Conversion in the New Testament*. Philadelphia, PA: Fortress Press.

Gnisci, Jacopo. 2020. "Constructing Kingship in Early Solomonic Ethiopia: The David and Solomon Portraits in the Juel-Jensen Psalter." *Art Bulletin* 102.4: 7–36.

Gori, Alessandro. 2020. "Islamic Cultural Traditions of Medieval Ethiopia and Eritrea." In *A Companion to Medieval Ethiopia and Eritrea*, edited by Samantha Kelly, 142–61. Leiden: Brill.

Grasso, Valentina. 2023. *Pre-Islamic Arabia: Societies, Politics, Cults and Identities during Late Antiquity*. Cambridge: Cambridge University Press.

Haaland, G., and R. Haaland. 2007. "God of War, Worldly Ruler, and Craft Specialists in the Meroitic Kingdom of Sudan: Inferring Social Identity from Material Remains." *Journal of Social Archaeology* 7.3: 372–92.

Hahn, Wolfgang. 2000. "Askumite Numismatics: A Critical Survey of Recent Research." *Revue Numismatique* 6.155: 281–311.

2016. "The Numismatic Heritage of Aksum: Coinage as a Multilateral Source in Studying Cultural History." *Ityopis: Northeast African Journal of Social Sciences and Humanities* 2: 48–58.

Hatke, George. 2011. "Africans in Arabia Felix: Aksumite Relations with Himyar in the Sixth Century C.E." PhD thesis, Princeton University.

2013. *Aksum and Nubia: Warfare, Commerce, and Political Fictions in Ancient Northeast Africa*. New York: New York University Press.

Heng, Geraldine. 2021. *The Global Middle Ages: An Introduction*. Cambridge: Cambridge University Press.

Horton, Robin. 1971. "African Conversion." *Africa: Journal of the International African Institute* 41.2: 85–108.

Huntingford, G. W. B., ed. 1965. *The Glorious Victories of Amda Seyon, King of Ethiopia*. Oxford: Oxford University Press.

Ibn Ḥawqal. 1964. *Ibn Hauqal – Configuration de La Terre (Kitab Surat al-Ard)*. Edited by Johannes Kramers and Goeje Wiet. Beirut: Commission Internationale pour la Traduction des Chefs-d'OEuvre.

Insoll, Timothy. 2001. "Dahlak Kebir, Eritrea: From Aksumite to Ottoman." *Adumatu* 3: 39–50.

2021. "Marine Shell Working at Harlaa, Ethiopia, and the Implications for Red Sea Trade." *Journal of African Archaeology* 19.1: 1–24.

2023. "Archaeological Perspectives on Contacts between Cairo and Eastern Ethiopia in the 12th to 15th Centuries." *Journal of the Economic and Social History of the Orient* 66.1–2: 154–205.

Insoll, Timothy, Nadia Khalaf, Rachel MacLean, Hannah Parsons-Morgan, Nicholas Tait, Jane Gaastra, Alemseged Beldados, Alexander J. E. Pryor, Laura Evis, and Laure Dussubieux. 2021. "Material Cosmopolitanism: The Entrepot of Harlaa as an Islamic Gateway to Eastern Ethiopia." *Antiquity* 95.380: 487–507.

Jeffery, Arthur. 2007. *The Foreign Vocabulary of the Qur'an*. Leiden: Brill.

Kaplan, Steven. 1982. "Ezana's Conversion Reconsidered." *Journal of Religion in Africa* 13.2: 101–9.

1984. *The Monastic Holy Man and the Christianization of Early Solomonic Ethiopia*. Wiesbaden: Franz Steiner.

Krebs, Verena. 2019. "Crusading Threats? Ethiopian–Egyptian Relations in the 1440s." In *Les Croisades en Afrique. XIII–XVIe Siècles*, edited by Benjamin Weber, 245–74. Toulouse: Presses Universitaires du Midi.

2021. *Medieval Ethiopian Kingship, Craft, and Diplomacy with Latin Europe*. Chur: Palgrave.

Kropp, Manfred. 1988. "The Śərʿatä Gəbr: A Mirror View of Daily Life at the Ethiopian Royal Court in the Middle Ages." *Northeast African Studies* 10.2–3: 51–87.

———. 1999. "'Glücklich, wer vom Weib geboren, dessen Tage doch kurzbemessen!' Die altäthiopische Grabinschrift, datiert auf den 23. Dezember 873 n. Chr." *Oriens Christianus* 83: 162–76.

Lepage, Claude. 2006. "Entre Aksum et Lalibela: Les Églises du Sud-Est du Tigray (IXe–XIIe s.) en Éthiopie." *Comptes Rendus des Séances de l'Académie des Inscriptions et Belles-Lettres* 150.1: 9–39.

Lepage, Claude, and Jacques Mercier. 2005. *Art Éthiopien: Les Églises Historiques du Tigray*. Paris: Éditions Recherche sur les Civilisations.

Levine, Donald N. 2000. *Greater Ethiopia: The Evolution of a Multiethnic Society*. Chicago, IL: University of Chicago Press.

Loiseau, Julien. 2019a. "Abyssinia at Al-Azhar: Muslim Students from the Horn of Africa in Late Medieval Cairo." *Northeast African Studies* 19.1: 61–84.

———. 2019b. "The Ḥaṭī and the Sultan: Letters and Embassies from Abyssinia to the Mamluk Court." In *Mamlūk Cairo, a Crossroads for Embassies: Studies on Diplomacy and Diplomatics*, edited by Frédéric Bauden and Malika Dekkiche, 638–57. Leiden: Brill.

———. 2020a. "Chrétiens d'Égypte, Musulmans d'Éthiopie: Protection des Communautés et Relations Diplomatiques entre le Sultanat Mamelouk et le Royaume Salomonien (ca 1270–1516)." *Médiévales* 79: 37–68.

———. 2020b. "Retour à Bilet: Un Cimetière Musulman Médiéval du Tigray Oriental." *Bulletin d'Études Orientales* 67.1: 59–96.

Loiseau, Julien, Simon Dorso, Yves Gleize, David Ollivier, Deresse Ayenachew, Hiluf Berhe, Amélie Chekroun, and Bertrand Hirsch. 2021. "Bilet and the Wider World: New Insights into the Archaeology of Islam in Tigray." *Antiquity* 95.380: 508–29.

Lusini, Gianfrancesco. 2002. "Christians and Moslems in Eastern Tigray up to the XIV C." *Studi Magrebini* 25: 245–52.

Marrassini, Paolo. 2007. "Kəbrä Nägäśt." In *Encyclopedia Aethiopica*, edited by Siegbert Uhlig, 3, He-N: 364–68.

Marshall, Michael H., Henry F. Lamb, Sarah J. Davies, Melanie J. Leng, Zelalem Kubsa, Mohammed Umer, and Charlotte Bryant. 2009. "Climatic Change in Northern Ethiopia during the Past 17,000 Years: A Diatom and Stable Isotope Record from Lake Ashenge." *Palaeogeography, Palaeoclimatology, Palaeoecology* 279.1: 114–27.

Martinez d'Alos-Moner, Andreu. 2015. *Envoys of a Human God: The Jesuit Mission to Christian Ethiopia, 1557–1632*. Leiden: Brill.

Massa, Serena, and Nelly Cattaneo. 2020. "Adulis (Eritrea): Criticità e Peculiarità di un Sito Complesso nel Corno d'Africa." *Archeologia e Calcolatori* 31.2: 45–57.

Matthews, Derek, and Antonio Mordini. 1959. "The Monastery of Debra Damo, Ethiopia." *Archaeologia* 97 Second Series, 47: 1–58.

Mekouria, T. T. 1981. "Christian Aksum." In *General History of Africa II: Ancient Civilizations of Africa*, edited by G. Mokhtar, 401–22. Berkeley: University of California Press.

Mercier, Jacques, and Claude Lepage. 2012. *Lalibela: Christian Art of Ethiopia, the Monolithic Churches and Their Treasures*. London: Paul Holberton Publishing.

Migne, Jacques-Paul. 1849. *Patrologiae Cursus Completus: Series Latina.* Vol. 21. Paris: Garnier Freres.

Mitchell, Stephen, and Peter van Nuffelen, eds. 2010. *Monotheism between Pagans and Christians in Late Antiquity.* Walpole, MA: Peeters.

Mordini, Antonio. 1957. "Un Tissu Musulman du Moyen Âge Provenant du Couvent de Dabra Dāmmò." Annales d'Éthiopie 2: 75–79.

1960. "Gli Aurei di Kushāna del Convento di Dabra Dāmmò: Un'indizio [*sic*] sui Rapporti Commerciali fra l'India e l'Etiopia nei Primi Secoli dell'era Volgare." In *Atti del Convegno Internazionale di Studi Etiopici (Roma 2–4 Aprile 1959)*, 249–54. Roma: Accademia Nazionale dei Lincei.

Muehlbauer, Mikael. 2021. "From Stone to Dust: The Life of the Kufic-Inscribed Frieze of Wuqro Cherqos in Tigray, Ethiopia." *Muqarnas Online* 38.1: 1–34.

2023a. "An African 'Constantine' in the Twelfth Century: The Architecture of the Early Zagwe Dynasty and Egyptian Episcopal Authority." *Gesta* 62.2: 127–152.

2023b. *Bastions of the Cross: Medieval Rock-Cut Cruciform Churches of Tigray, Ethiopia*. Washington, DC: Dumbarton Oaks Research Library and Collection.

Munro-Hay, Stuart C. 1982. "The Foreign Trade of Aksumite Port of Adulis." *Azania* 17: 107–25.

1991. *Aksum: An African Civilization of Late Antiquity.* Edinburgh: Edinburgh University Press.

1997. *Ethiopia and Alexandria: The Metropolitan Episcopacy of Ethiopia.* Warszawa–Wiesbaden: ZAŚ PAN.

2001. "A Sixth Century Kebra Nagast?" *Annales d'Éthiopie* 17.1: 43–58.

Munro-Hay, Stuart, and Rodolfo Fattovich. 2003. "Aksum." In *Encyclopaedia Aethiopica*, edited by Siegbert Uhlig, I: 173b–83. Wiesbaden: Harrassowitz.

Munro-Hay, Stuart, and Denis Nosnitsin. 2005. "Danʾel, Ḥaṣani." In *Encyclopaedia Aethiopica*, edited by Siegbert Uhlig, II: 84a–85a. Wiesbaden: Harrassowitz.

Parsons-Morgan, Hannah. 2023. "Chinese Ceramic Consumption in Medieval Ethiopia: An Archaeological Perspective." *Orientations* 54.3: 34–42.

Phillipson, David. 2003. "Aksum: An Archaeological Introduction and Guide." *Azania: Archaeological Research in Africa* 38.1: 1–68.

   2014. *Foundations of an African Civilisation: Aksum & the Northern Horn, 1000 BC–AD 1300*. Woodbridge: James Currey.

Philostorgius. 2007. *Church History*. Translated by Philip R. Amidon. Atlanta, GA: Society of Biblical Literature.

Playne, Beatrice. 1954. *St. George for Ethiopia*. London: Constable.

Pogossian, Zaroui. 2021. "Armeno-Aethiopica in the Middle Ages: Geography, Tales of Christianization, Calendars, and Anti-Dyophysite Polemics in the First Millennium." *Aethiopica* 24: 104–40.

Portella, Mario Alexis, and Abraham Buruk Woldegaber. 2012. *Abyssinian Christianity: The First Christian Nation*. Edited by Brendan Pringle. BP Editing.

Power, Timothy. 2009. "The Expansion of Muslim Commerce in the Red Sea Basin, c. AD 833–969." In *Connected Hinterlands. Proceedings of Red Sea Project IV*, edited by Lucy Blue, John Cooper, Ross Thomas, and Julian Whitewright, 111–18. Oxford: Archaeopress.

Pryor, A. J. E., T. Insoll, and L. Evis. 2020. "Laser Ablation Strontium Isotope Analysis of Human Remains from Harlaa and Sofi, Eastern Ethiopia, and the Implications for Islamisation and Mobility." *STAR: Science & Technology of Archaeological Research* 6.1: 113–36.

Raven, Wim. 1988. "Some Early Islamic Texts on the Negus of Abyssinia." *Journal of Semitic Studies* 33.2: 197–218.

Robin, Christian Julien. 1989. "La Premiere Intervention Abyssine en Arabie Meridionale (de 200 a 270 de l'Ere Chretienne Environ)." In *Proceedings of the Eighth International Conference of Ethiopian Studies*, edited by Taddese Beyene, 2: 147–62. Addis Ababa: Institute of Ethiopian Studies.

   2010. "L'Antiquité." In *Routes d'Arabie: Archéologie et Histoire du Royaume d'Arabie Séoudite*, edited by Ali Ibrahim Al-Ghabban, Béatrice André-Salvini, and Françoise Demange, 80–99. Paris: Musée du Louvre.

   2015. "Ḥimyar, Aksūm, and Arabia Deserta in Late Antiquity: The Epigraphic Evidence." In *Arabs and Empires Before Islam*, edited by Greg Fisher, 127–71. Oxford: Oxford University Press.

Rufinus. 1997. *The Church History of Rufinus of Aquileia: Books 10 and 11*. Translated by Philip R. Amidon. Oxford: Oxford University Press.

Rukuni, Rugare. 2020. "Religious Statecraft: Constantinianism in the Figure of Nagashi Kaleb." *Hervormde Teologiese Studies* 76.4: 1–12.

2021. "Negus Ezana: Revisiting the Christianisation of Aksum." *Verbum et Ecclesia* 42.1: 1–11.

Sāwīris ibn al-Muqaffaʿ. 1948. *History of the Patriarchs of the Egyptian Church: Known as the History of the Holy Church, Volume 2, Part 2: Khaël III–Senouti II (A.D. 880–1066) by Sawīrus Ibn al-Mukaffaʾ, Bishop of Al-Asmunin.* Edited by ʿAbd al-Masih Yassā. Translated by Aziz Suryal Atiya and Oswald Hugh Edward Burmester. Cairo: Société d'archéologie copte.

1970. *History of the Patriarchs of the Egyptian Church: Known as the History of the Holy Church, Volume 3, Part 2: Mark III–John VI (A.D. 1167–1216).* Edited by ʿAbd al-Masih Yassā. Translated by Aziz Suryal Atiya and Oswald Hugh Edward Burmester. Cairo: Société d'archéologie copte.

Schneider, Madeleine. 1967. "Stèles Funéraires Arabes de Quiha." *Annales d'Éthiopie* 7: 107–22.

1983. *Stèles Funéraires Musulmanes des Îles Dahlak (Mer Rouge).* 2 Vols. Cairo: Imprimerie de l'Institut Français d'Archéologie Orientale.

Seignobos, Robin. 2020. "Pouvoirs Chrétiens et Musulmans, de la Corne de l'Afrique à la Vallée du Nil (Xie–Xve Siècle)." *Médiévales* 79: 5–14.

Sergew Hable Selassie. 1972. *Ancient and Medieval Ethiopian History to 1270.* Addis Ababa: United Printers.

Simmons, Adam. 2022. *Nubia, Ethiopia, and the Crusading World, 1095–1402.* New York: Routledge.

Smidt, Wolbert G. C. 2004. "Eine arabische Inschrift in Kwiḥa, Tigray." In *Studia Aethiopica in Honour of Siegbert Uhlig on the Occasion of His 65th Birthday*, edited by Verena Böll, Denis Nosnitsin, Thomas Rave, Wolbert Smidt, and Evgenia Sokolinskaia, 259–68. Wiesbaden: Harrassowitz.

2009. "Eine weitere arabische Inschrift von der osttigrayischen Handelsroute: Hinweis auf eine muslimische Kultstätte in der 'Dunklen Periode'?" *Aethiopica* 12: 126–35.

2010. "Another Unknown Arabic Inscription from the Eastern Tigrayan Trade Route." *Orbis Aethiopicus* 13: 179–91.

Smidt, Wolbert, and Alessandro Gori. 2010. "Ottoman Empire, Relations with The." In *Encyclopaedia Aethiopica*, edited by Siegbert Uhlig and Alessandro Bausi, IV: 74b–81a. Wiesbaden: Harrassowitz.

Stenhouse, Paul Lester, and Richard Pankhurst, eds. 2005. *Futūḥ Al-Ḥabaša: The Conquest of Abyssinia.* Hollywood, LA: Tsehai Publishers.

Stephenson, Paul. 2009. *Constantine: Roman Emperor, Christian Victor.* New York: Overlook Press.

Stroumsa, Guy G. 2015. *The Making of the Abrahamic Religions in Late Antiquity*. Oxford: Oxford University Press.

Symes, Carol. 2011. "When We Talk About Modernity." *American Historical Review* 116.3: 715–26.

Taddesse Tamrat. 1970. "The Abbots of Däbrä-Hayq, 1248–1535." *Journal of Ethiopian Studies* 8.1: 87–117.

1972. *Church and State in Ethiopia, 1270–1527*. Oxford: Clarendon Press.

Tsegay Berhe Gebre Libanos. 2005. "Däbrä Damo." In *Encyclopedia Aethiopica*, edited by Siegbert Uhlig, vol. 2, D-Ha: 17–20. Wiesbaden: Harassowitz.

Wion, Anaïs. 2020. "Medieval Ethiopian Economies: Subsistence, Global Trade and the Administration of Wealth." In *A Companion to Medieval Ethiopia and Eritrea*, edited by Samantha Kelly, 395–425. Leiden: Brill.

Woldekiros, Helina S. 2019. "The Route Most Traveled: The Afar Salt Trail, North Ethiopia." *Chungará (Arica)* 51: 95–110.

Wolska-Conus, Wanda, ed. 1962. *La Topographie Chrétienne de Cosmas Indicopleustès*. Paris: Presses Universitaires de France.

Yohannes Gebre Selassie. 2011. "Plague as a Possible Factor for the Decline and Collapse of the Aksumite Empire: A New Interpretation." *ITYOPIS – Northeast African Journal of Social Sciences and Humanities* 1: 36–61.

Zazzaro, Chiara, Clément Flaux, Alfredo Carannante, and Christophe Morhange. 2015. "Adulis in Its Regional Maritime Context: A Preliminary Report of the 2015 Field Season." *Newsletter Di Archeologia CISA* 6: 279–94.

Cambridge Elements ☰

The Global Middle Ages

Geraldine Heng
University of Texas at Austin

Geraldine Heng is Perceval Professor of English and Comparative Literature at the University of Texas, Austin. She is the author of *The Invention of Race in the European Middle Ages* (2018) and *England and the Jews: How Religion and Violence Created the First Racial State in the West* (2018), both published by Cambridge University Press, as well as *Empire of Magic: Medieval Romance and the Politics of Cultural Fantasy* (2003, Columbia). She is the editor of *Teaching the Global Middle Ages* (2022, MLA), coedits the University of Pennsylvania Press series, RaceB4Race: Critical Studies of the Premodern, and is working on a new book, Early Globalisms: The Interconnected World, 500-1500 CE. Originally from Singapore, Heng is a Fellow of the Medieval Academy of America, a member of the Medievalists of Color, and Founder and Co-director, with Susan Noakes, of the Global Middle Ages Project: www.globalmiddleages.org.

Susan J. Noakes
University of Minnesota–Twin Cities

Susan J. Noakes is Professor of French and Italian at the University of Minnesota–Twin Cities, where she also serves as Chair of the Department of French and Italian. For her many publications in French, Italian, and Comparative Literature, the University In 2009 named her Inaugural Chair in Arts, Design, and Humanities. Her most recent publication is an analysis of Salim Bachi's *L'Exil d'Ovide*, exploring a contemporary writer's reflection on his exile to Europe by comparing it to Ovid's exile to the Black Sea; it appears in *Salim Bachi*, edited by Agnes Schaffhauser, published in Paris by Harmattan in 2020.

Lynn Ramey
Vanderbilt University

Lynn Ramey is Professor of French and Cinema and Media Arts at Vanderbilt University and Chair of the Department of French and Italian. She is the author of *Jean Bodel: An Introduction* (2024, University Press of Florida), *Black Legacies: Race and the European Middle Ages* (2014, University Press of Florida), and *Christian, Saracen and Genre in Medieval French Literature* (2001, Routledge). She is currently working on recreations of medieval language, literature, and culture in video games for which she was awarded an NEH digital humanities advancement grant in 2022.

About the Series

Elements in the Global Middle Ages is a series of concise studies that introduce researchers and instructors to an uncentered, interconnected world, c. 500-1500 CE. Individual Elements focus on the globe's geographic zones, its natural and built environments, its cultures, societies, arts, technologies, peoples, ecosystems, and lifeworlds.

Cambridge Elements ☰

The Global Middle Ages

Printed in the United States
by Baker & Taylor Publisher Services